A COLOURFUL LIFE

SAOIRSE WELLAND

A CIP catalogue record for this book is available from the British Library.

Publisher: Lottie Publishing

ISBN: 978-1-0369-0267-4

www.searchingforsersh.wordpress.com

DEDICATION

Hayley, Thank you for reminding me to fall in love with writing all over again, without you this wouldn't be possible.

Love you Croc xxx

CONTENTS

ABOUT THE AUTHOR

Saoirse Welland is young, not yet thirty years old and yet she has overcome so much in her young life.

This is her story. Painful to read, it is harder to live, but she has lived it and continues daily to build a better life from the tragedy already endured.

Saoirse appreciates the power of sharing her experience with fellow alcoholics and anorexics. Through shared experience, she has learnt the power of perspective and that she, in fact, isn't alone.

She hopes that her story will resonate with individuals who are either in active addiction or embarking on their recovery journey. Equally, her shared story will alleviate some of the shame and guilt associated with behaviours and actions one engages with whilst actively pursuing addiction.

Since writing this book, Saoirse has lost her dear companion, Lottie, her darling sausage dog. Something that signifies so much more than a pet, but a confidant who held witness to all of her highs and lows.

One day at a time, she maintains her sobriety and endeavours to share with others what was freely given to her.

FOREWORD

By Catherine Williamson, Podcaster and Author of 'Gobsmacked'

I was catapulted into Saoirse's life on a terrible, unimaginable, and tragic day back on December 1st, 2011. The death of her cheeky, charismatic, and captivating brother Tiarnan, a school friend of my daughter Alice, is a day I will never forget. Over the years, I kept an eye out for news of the family. Then, one day three years ago, I saw a Facebook post from Saoirse. Her writing was extraordinary and compelling. Her searing account of the terrible events that had unfolded in her life since that dark December day knocked me sideways. To imagine that the Welland family had so very nearly lost another member in a road accident was terrible to contemplate.

I could see that Saoirse was a gifted communicator, so I reached out to her and invited her on my Gobsmacked! podcast. As I stared across the mic into her beautiful eyes that day, I was once again floored by her story and her articulation. To now have the privilege of writing the foreword for her book is something I will hold dear. I marvel and applaud her courage–that instead of cowering away in a corner, engulfed in shame, this courageous fighter has bravely stuck her head above the parapet, putting her thoughts, heart, and soul out there for us. I am so very proud of her and await, with anticipation, as her talented self rockets skyward. I invite you now to be moved, floored and captivated too.

PREFACE

Here goes nothing, it's time to make a start with this old book as opposed to procrastinating for another foreseeable few months. Kaleo is blasting on the TV, a bit of 'Glass House' to get me pumped for this endeavour. Lottie, my favourite sausage, is on my lap, licking me eagerly to get me started.

Where the fuck do I begin? I could mull over the standard 'past' small print about my upbringing and woe is me, but that never gets me anywhere. Instead, I'll depict the relevant pieces as and when it's appropriate.

Sat glaring at me is 'Glorious Rock Bottom' by Bryony Gordon - I'm thinking how the fuck can I compete with a book like this, and I'm still yet to read it! Shall I start with the bottle or with the food, gosh I can see the word vomit sprawling across these pages - you're in for a ride of some type anyhow.

Rides have got me thinking, I used to think I was a wild ride when drinking, I was the riot, firecracker if you will. In actual fact nothing could be further from the truth. Give me a bump of cocaine and I was every man's wet dream... I truly came alive with Pablo Escobar's finest.

Circle back many moons ago, I was with my ex - and who would have been better suited for me than him. Two addicts in active addiction were a recipe for disaster. I've heard the term 'enabler' and we equally were the other's. As my drinking spiralled so did my nasal consumption of cocaine, my moral compass skewed.

That was mind altering substances for you, and a shit heap of ego entangled. I used to be anti-drugs, I would convince myself I was so I didn't appear to be a sheep. God forbid I followed the crowd. In fact, I never felt 'part of' growing up, I never felt at home with a group of friends, I felt alone...

This brings me back to the old school days, I felt like a fish out of water. I did have my own little tribes over the years, the first fell apart after the death of my dear friend Ruby, she sadly passed with cancer. Just 13 years old.

This was my first introduction to grief and loss, losing her at 13 was like losing a right arm - it was so very noticeable and foreign. I don't know if a 'known' death is easier to grieve, as you live on borrowed time with that person, rather than a sudden one.

After her passing my friendship group changed, I was close to X and Y, God did we have some good times. X was blessed with the upper hand of looking older, thus getting served for alcohol came naturally to her. We would spend our nights out drinking in the park; attending parties; or drinking at X's.

Every moment was a cause for celebration or to commiserate, boredom was my favourite excuse to use. I remember being with the girls down the park and downing Frosty Jacks - I had to hold my nose for the entire duration as I gulped it down. It's safe to say I was violently sick as the night drew to a conclusion.

I needed to meet that forsaken magic feeling I encountered after my first sip of alcohol. I best describe it as a warm blanket on a cold day, and nothing measures up to that. Nothing though, could beat that initial sense of confidence; freeness and safety. It was a constant chase, a mission I made my own.

I couldn't tell you the exact age I first tasted the devil's juice, but my parents, both 'normal' drinkers, never shied us away from it. We were encouraged to have Schloer as our kiddies' alternative to wine, but I always ensured I got a sip of wine to wash it down with.

An Irish Catholic will always be proud to tell you they're an Irish Catholic, so as one I thought I'd mention it - ha! Believe it or not, the only incentive for attending church was the 'blood of Christ'. It replicated a similar taste to wine; I remember a priest once grabbing the chalice off me to stop me from drinking it all. To this day I still don't know if it has any alcohol contents/traces.

My love for our trips to the south of France were solely for the Châteaux trips, yes wine tasting. I would sip on fine dessert wines at the tender age of 8. Roland was our wine guy in the South, my parents would book trips to individually go and collect cases of wine from him - there was always booze in the house, and plenty of it.

So, after losing Ruby, it was fully accessible, a comfort blanket if you will. That's when the drinking became secretive, and I found a new outlet for those unimaginable emotions I had just met ...

Chapter 1

MAMMA DEAREST

"Behaviour is the language of trauma. Children will show you before they tell you that they are in distress"

Micere Keels

Chickatees' - Tayto's best crisp to this day, and one of my favourite things to indulge. They were the pinnacle of my short upbringing in Ireland. That, and the Houdini shit I would pull with the neighbours. Yes, call me a magician if you will, I have fond memories of jumping over the wall between ours and the neighbours, and playing hide and seek.

Either of our parents would be knocking the others' door in a desperate attempt to get us home for dinner. It was a blast consisting of the happy ingredients to secure a happy childhood. I'll never forget my auntie coming armed with Chickatees on one of her frequent visits.

It was the essence of pure bliss, I can even recall our gardener, but my dad was missing, he was back in the UK working. If only I had known what I did now, how married to his job he was, but then again, the poor guy had a family to provide for. I'm utterly grateful for the benefits I have reaped as a result of all his hard work.

As the years began to pass, my mother's mental health began to deteriorate as did her treatment towards me and our family unit. She was a narcissist at the very least, a woman who possessed an acid tongue and a good wallop. She was only invested in herself, her Jaffa Cakes and the entire contents of Sky TV.

It's difficult to reminisce about those torturous times because she truly scared and hurt me, and this isn't to play the victim. I was in fight and flight, my sympathetic system was through the roof, and it caused me to fall back on wine and restrict food.

She failed as a mother when I was 4 years old. I was sexually abused by a neighbour, his version of 'Mummy's and Daddy's' with an evil twist. It all took place in my playroom, door shut whilst she pottered around the house none the wiser. Until, one day she opened the door, and my first encounter with trauma was revealed.

But how does a 4-year-old articulate they've been raped on several occasions? There aren't any words, well there wasn't in my dialogue. Instead of going to the police, my parents spoke with his parents, my mother still insists this was to prevent me from going on a 'sex victims' list - there's no such thing.

The weeks passed by with no sign of the neighbour, my stomach was in my arse. The longer the periods in between incidents meant the bigger the consequences... the more pain I would be subject to.

In pure fear, I threw my football over the fence, in hope he would come over and get the deed over with, but nothing. I was petrified of the dark (it always happened with the blinds closed); I frequently wet the bed; and would often share a bed with my parents.

To relieve myself of the induced anxiety and fear I felt, I compensated with food restriction. Mother always battled with her weight; I noticed the difference in her mood when she was successfully losing weight. She was happier. I acknowledged that this was mostly when she ate salad.

My love for starvation commenced, fuelled by secrecy and lies. I just wanted to feel happier and safe again. As a way to cope I began to hide my snacks; eat less at meal times and sometimes would ONLY eat 3 strands of grass a day. Grass was my substitute for salad, it was easily accessible in the garden. I linked salad with weight loss - the evidence was there, my mother was happier, so surely I would be?

It alleviated the emotional turmoil I was faced with, suppressing those unwanted emotions, giving me power and control over the situation, something I seek even to this day. I needed to change how I felt, and at the tender age of four food was my best bet.

My family was notorious for making geographical moves. This initial trauma occurred in Colchester, after we (my parents, two sisters and I) had moved back from Ireland.

My beautiful brother Tiarnan was born in Colchester, and with great relief we moved to Shropshire where the baby was born. It was music to my ears knowing we were leaving the epicentre of my new found hell. To be a million miles away from my perpetrator was a blessing, no more pain was to be endured. Little did I know...

Mother was never satisfied as an individual, a touch of the ISM's (I, Self, Myself - me, me, me) if you will. We had to have the biggest houses; best clothes and huge parties. It was all about setting the perfect impression to the outside world, our family members joked we were The Von Trapp's!

We were the most well-mannered kids on the block, a joy to be around, but little did anyone know the monster we were living with. Someone who spat with pure venom, I've never seen someone so enraged.

Upon reflection, her turbulent relationship with her in-laws should have been an indicator of how she managed and dealt with situations. They always appeared to be at logger heads with each other, nothing was ever good enough for them.

I remember at 4 ripping up a cheque from my auntie, I strongly felt it was wrong to receive money from someone I had hardly seen, let alone knew. My grandparents (Dad's side) witnessed me do this, and Christ it was like Dunkirk, albeit I knew my mother was defending me for a change. I was a young bambino trying to make sense of what started to seem like a dark world.

To add to matters, living back in the UK meant seeing less of my Irish grandparents, the two people I hold so dearly to my heart. I remember periods of minimal contact with them because there had been some type of disagreement.

It was my grandfather who came over when Mother walked out on my sister's 13th birthday. Yep, you read that right, she just got up and left one day, my heart broke for my sister. My granda was livid, he couldn't fathom this behaviour or what she was becoming.

Her estranged relationship with her family, and us, was to be experienced by years of no communication until my grandparents wanted to see her. They had some shares for each of their children, and as usual wanted to treat everyone the same. It killed them inside, the lack of conversation upon the discomfort of her accepting their money with little to no gratitude.

Mother dearest was full of resentment, she was engulfed with anger and pure paranoia. After Ruby passed all bets were off, I never knew what version of her I'd get. It brings me back to when my sister and I were drinking whiskey in our bedroom over a Ben & Jerry's, unbeknown to Mother. She even knocked the door and for once was totally oblivious. Gosh, I can feel the warmth of the whiskey trickle down my throat, that satisfying feeling.

Ruby Lee was one of a kind, my darling best friend who passed away from Neuroblastoma. In a bid to raise funds for her dream holiday to Florida, she'd arranged a ramble walk. My mother wasn't best impressed, 'she only wants to know you when she wants something' was her attitude. It was soul destroying for a then 13-year-old me to hear such bullshit, and to have no backbone to stand up for her friend.

I'll never forget when Ruby returned home from Florida, she ran up to me happy as anything and in hand was a Hilary Duff tour DVD, I never told her I had a copy of it. I still have it to this day, and that reminds me I must watch it. I was Hilary Duff mad as a kid, my parents paid for me and my sisters to see her at the Hammersmith Apollo, I cried so much, in disbelief I was in the same room as her. Her bouncer passed me a signed autograph of hers, I was that obsessed I wrote my English speech on the experience.

Ruby was sadly never going to get better, so us girls made the most of our thirteenths. We separately hosted our parties, Ruby had a jacuzzi party, the gang were amazed at it, I remember thinking how cool we were. I had a makeup party where we designed acrylic nails and had little mini treatments. My mother had always done nice things for show, it was one of her greatest attributes, she'd host lavish parties for everyone else but us.

I will never forget the last time I saw Ruby, she was on her death bed, wired up to all sorts of machines and medication. I promised her I would stay in contact with her parents, to keep an eye on them, and I'm privileged to say I have kept this promise for the last 15 years.

I miss her terribly; a constant thought is 'what would we be like today?'; something that will never be answered. I feel a void for her, she was an energy you couldn't but love, she was an angel who was taken too early. She was the first person I ever lost, and I didn't know how to digest grief and all its stages. That's when the drinking really revved up, it was easier to forget, with the numbness vodka brought, than to remember.

The one thing Ruby was queen of was fancying boys, she would regularly ask lads out. I used to admire her confidence and vivaciousness for life. She simply didn't give a shit, she had balls of steel and she oozed everything I wanted. I was in pure awe of her.

It wasn't until Ruby passed that I was used as the pawn in Mother's game, she blamed her passing for my 'rebellious' streak. In actual fact, I was reacting to my mother's horrific behaviour, it was as if I was screaming, praying to be heard and listened to.

Over time Mother became reluctant to do household chores, even her personal hygiene deteriorated. I was constantly cleaning, to the point of washing walls and tidying up before Dad got home. He worked crazy long hours and would often return back to her watching TV and us causing a riot.

Dad was at fault too; he was just as responsible for the turmoil us kids endured. He chose to work and turn a blind eye to the shit going on at home, so I had no choice but to step up. The chaos of our family life was about to step up a gear...

Her obsession around crash diets was to reappear, we went on to try several 'family' health kicks all to compensate for the excessive weight she had put on. She was supposed to be a role model, losing 11 stone in under a year and a half.

I emulated her behaviours, sneaking her weight loss shakes for my own personal use. I craved starvation, and with it came the 'light weight' version of me. I could get pissed at a faster rate. She claimed she done this because us kids were being scrutinised at school... I can't weigh in on that, it's a distant memory. Pardon the pun. Yep, you read it right folks, an astronomical amount of weight which caught the eye of the media, she featured in Red magazine headlining how her poor children were bullied as a result of her weight.

In fact, we were bullied, bullied for having a 24 stone mother, but it was hard to digest the martyr spiel she had reeled out in her magazine debut. We were so accustomed to 'JLS' (J's Lazy Saturdays/Sundays) where she would consume ample amounts of Jaffa cakes and binge watch Sky TV. Not one iota or glimmer of that person was mentioned in the article.

As her food remained out of control, her control was quickly passed onto us. She would tell us what to wear, manipulate one against the other four and so forth. One morning my sister and I woke early to be welcomed with the news our parents were getting divorced;

this was the first my dad had heard of it. She scared the living daylights out of us, we didn't want to come from a broken family no matter how scarring her actions and words were.

The only wholesome, happy memory I had with her was when I went to see Hilary Duff in concert. As already mentioned, Hilary was my ride or die, I had all of her Lizzie McGuire clothes; Stuff by Duff; concert DVDs and general merchandise. It was one of the few moments I seen my mother in a kind, maternal light. It's a memory I'll treasure to my dying day.

Normally we'd be expected to keep up appearances like attending church religiously every Sunday. She would threaten to section me following one of my angry outbursts, I'd refuse to go to church because I never believed in it. I always chose to have a private relationship with my God (one based on my own understanding).

It was pure torture, having to read on a weekly basis, being confined to the type of clothing she chose for us. A routine I did not want to engage with, I believed most of that congregation lived in fear of God - surely that's the opposite of what religion is about?

In other news, the worst was once when she left us in the middle of the day, and two men turned up in a van. As they posted something through the door, they continued to look around the outside of the house. We were horrified, fearful they'd break in and take us. Thankfully they soon left, it was just a weird set-up to be frank.

Mother would also sit in the car and write up 'notes' of incidents she felt she fell victim to. She would record us on her phone, selecting when to do so, so as to appear as 'Mother of the Year'. It was all on her terms, she would pause the recordings when she'd respond (more like react) with her pure venom.

She'd gaslight me to fuck, I was the initial one who endured her nastier side. Before Dad came home one evening, I was in conflict with her over something, and she went for me. My only option was to smash crockery all around me to create a barrier from her. She went mad and so did Dad. He was tired upon returning home, finding a shit tip was the last thing he needed, bless him.

Rewind the tape, we were in Ireland as a family, driving Dad to the airport so he could fly back for work. A car hit us as we crossed a crossroads, the car spun numerous times and stopped as it hit an electrical pole. I'll never forget that day, my siblings and I thought Dad had died as the paramedics took him off with oxygen on a stretcher. I remember someone from the petrol station opposite, running out with Chupa Chups, insisting we have one to help with our blood sugars.

Off to the hospital we separately went, I had a cut on my foot, my sibling's had various minor injuries as well. It was surreal, my mother had broken her foot and was bruised all over. Dad came to and thankfully was ok.

I believe that was the event that shook the apple cart, the one that really changed things for the worst. I only learnt of the extent of her injuries years later, but if I was to pinpoint where she deteriorated it would be from there.

CHAPTER 2

ROSÉ TO RHIANNA

"Sudden loss of a loved one, as if ambushed by fate, awakens an endless pain, birthing a lesion which is granted an unwelcome immortality"

Amit Jotwani

Fast forward to my first heavy encounter with alcohol, I was in Year 8 and it involved a litre bottle of blue label vodka. I'd taken it from my parent's famous 'drinks cabinet', it was the holy grail, full of every spirit you could desire. A friend was staying for a sleep over, and I thought it would be the perfect time to experiment with the heavy shit. I was so intoxicated I found myself rolling around in my piss, this wasn't going to be the last time for sure. Gosh that feeling was like a warm blanket on a cold day.

All my inhibitions were skewed but not as much as my friend's, so much so, that the paramedics were called. She was being horrendously sick, and once my parents were informed, my mother's entrance came with a large slap across my back. Thankfully my friend was ok, she just rode it out, the following day we sat at the dining table, eating pasta as she still remained pissed. This was very much to my mother's annoyance.

This didn't throw me off drinking, in fact it exasperated it. Mother dearest was full of resentment, she was engulfed with anger and pure paranoia. After Ruby passed all bets were off, I never knew what version of her I'd get. It became a reliable friend to me, always there in any given situation.

And so, as most youngsters' experiment, mine continued with friends; from smoking copious amounts of cigarettes over a couple of bottles of wine to drinking Frosty Jack's that a friend had gotten served with.

After a friend completed her acne medication, we even celebrated with a couple of bottles of wine, you see everything, even from that age, became about drinking. It was always a case of how as opposed to why. I had already begun to manipulate people around me; I was cunning with whom I drank, even from an early age.

It was oblivion I was seeking; it was a desirable feeling that was better than any parental love (which I rarely received). I always found that one drink was never enough, but now I'm sober I know one drink is too many and 100 isn't enough. I found a great distinction between oblivion and music, the essence of getting lost in the lyrics. They were moments I truly felt like I was listened to, that someone else was able to share in my experiences.

When I was younger, I felt it appropriate to experiment with marijuana, the first time was in the pissing rain. My friends had rolled the joints at theirs, and both of them were acting aggressively. I was utterly confused, all I knew was I was soaked through and through, I didn't feel anything during this escapade. I reckon it wasn't until the next time that I truly popped my weed cherry.

You see living with just Dad was a dream, we had a good system. He was always married to his job, but now I realise he was working extremely hard to provide a life for me and my siblings. There was a lot of freedom in his absence, although we lived in the middle of nowhere. My drinking became almost hidden in plain sight as a result of his minimal presence.

The relationship between me and my siblings remained good, we all got on, especially as we welcomed a nanny to our home. Asta would bring my brothers' to their primary school and cook for us all of an evening. She was a dream, a lady with so much love and insight, I felt truly blessed to have a healthy female figure around me.

There was one time when she caught me drinking rosé to Rihanna, I was of course in oblivion, singing my heart out to 'We found Love'. I was relating it to my then boy trouble and affairs of the heart. She gave me a disheartened look, one to say, 'there's no answer in the bottle, there's only pain'.

That moment stuck with me; it was the first time I really felt that uncomfortable knot in my stomach. The one that signified my drinking was not normal. It continued to be the 'elephant in the room', an unspoken topic which was never broached.

Before Asta came into our lives, Mother was still cohabiting with us, and the older I got the more I rebelled - the longer I was out of the house, the better. I would choose to get the later bus home to allow me time in town with my friends, but one time she caught me.

Mother was collecting my sister for an acupuncturist appointment and she saw me walking with friends away from the school gates. I ignored her, hoping I could discreetly continue to walk past the car, going unseen, but the woman never missed a trick.

She followed me, shouting from the car, demanding I get in it or else. I proceeded to walk, thinking she'd give over, but no, I was naive to think such a thing. She shouted in front of the 'cool' boys at school, the ones I would occasionally crush on. It was at that point I got in the car, she was screaming at me, I slapped her across the face from the passenger seat behind (yes, I'm not proud of my actions nor do I condone them), and BOOM. She screamed, 'I'm going to section you, you little bitch'.

Fear ran through my bones, she was a woman with power, possession and control. I soon quietened down, she dropped me and my sister at the acupuncturist, she had to go and collect my siblings. I took my opportunity; I seized the moment. As my sister had her session upstairs, I legged it, I met a friend and dossed around at the rec.

My phone continued to blow up, it rang consecutively for over an hour. It wasn't until she threatened to get the police involved that I finally waved the white flag, I gave her my location. She and Dad collected me, it was a relief to see him in the car, he was my safety blanket.

You see I was the scapegoat in her narcissistic game. At one point she accused me of being on drugs, at a time when I honestly wasn't using. I was at the age where I refused to be a 'sheep', I made a conscious decision to stay clear of narcotics, aside from the fags; they were an essential.

She sat Dad and I down and laid out her accusation, I immediately reacted to the situation, how dare she accuse me of such a thing! I was then brought to the GP to discuss these 'suspected' issues, I can't recall if I was drug tested or not, but even my dad knew it was a waste of time.

I thought my encounters with the police would be nil, I'll never forget my first. I was 14/15 years old, innocently returning home on the school bus, and I got a call from my brother. He was crying, he said, 'Saoirse, Mum has called the police, she's getting you arrested, and she said anyone over the age of 11 can be too'. He was perplexed with fear, thinking he'd be arrested too. The poor wee mite, I couldn't fathom what I'd be walking in on.

I called my aunties and Granny, they each assumed she was bluffing, this was her poker face, to yet again cause drama and fear amongst us. You see the night before, she done her usual, she lost her shit and went to slap me, but I slapped her first thinking it would at least stop her in her tracks. She claimed this slap caused her to see a 'white light'...

Upon getting home, she acted as if nothing was going on, my poor brothers' were distraught. I was upstairs on the phone between various calls with the extended family, and next thing you know the police arrived. I say police, but it was one copper, he was invited into the living room where they discussed at length, all I can assume, were her lies.

What I thought was his leaving ended up with me being recited my rights, being handcuffed in front of my crying siblings. My sister ran out after me, pleading for me not to go, she was quickly threatened with being arrested by the guy.

I was a minor being accompanied by one male police officer; something just didn't add up about this. He drove down the road, stopped and unhandcuffed me. He then took a detour and parked up at a garage for a while, I just referred to all the movies I watched. I had the right to remain silent and all that jazz.

We finally arrived at the cop shop... we drove in and I was brought through to custody. Everything, bracelets the lot were taken off me to minimise the risk of self-harm or suicide - it's just procedure. I was brought to my cell, my neighbour was a guy I had put a witness statement in for a few weeks prior, he had assaulted my friend at the park.

The door and shutter closed, it was just me and an iron bed, I was cold, clucking for a fag and a drink to take the edge off. All I could think about was how on earth I'd be able to escape if someone bombed the place? There was knock at my cell door, I was asked if I wanted a magazine, I thought 'sure' anything to pass the time.

Low and behold, one of them featured an article about Cheryl Cole's experience in a cell, it really highlighted how scared she was. The whole time I was praying that the place didn't get bombed, I didn't fancy spending my dying hours in an iron box.

Finally, my dad arrived and I was taken in for questioning, the sergeant was lovely, he was very understanding of our family situation. I received a 'verbal' slap on the wrist, I was reminded that if something like this was to happen again, I'd be arrested again. Dad got me some cheesy chips from the famous Viallis, and a 10 deck of fags, I chain smoked half of them before I got home.

We were perplexed by the events that unravelled, on my return home, the woman I called Mother, looked contrite. She was insistent that she was advised to take such action, that she knew the copper in charge and was certain of the outcome, that I wouldn't be arrested or charged.

I was almost in disbelief at what happened, sure I should never have slapped her, but I was defending myself against a 24 stone woman, a woman who was supposed to love and protect me. I couldn't continue being her physical punch bag, I was through with it. I was helpless, I was reactive rather than responsive.

To make matters worse, I was then collared for smoking by one of the I.T. teachers, he caught me, so this meant detention and a letter sent home. I told Dad prior to this, he already knew I was smoking, in fact he used to give me money to get cigarettes because I explained just how stressful our family life was, and how I'd been stealing money from him so a mate's mum could buy me them.

Once the letter arrived home, I had a sit-down meeting with the parents, Dad acted oblivious to all matters concerning my smoking. It was as if it was the first he was hearing of it. I sat and took the bollocking, desperate for a cigarette, I'm pretty sure I totally disassociated from it all. I had 'jist' brain, I was so beaten down with being her target. And what would cure the anxiety rush? but only a delicious sip of vodka and nicotine.

The worst was yet to come though, it was the summer before she vacated the family home. She had held our passports hostage at her solicitors, and in a time of desperate need, Dad booked the ferry for us to head over to Ireland to the extended family. Mother was initially unaware of this, we managed to secretly pack our bags and the car. Of course, she surely made a stark discovery.

In her newfound realisation, she tried to slash the tyres of the car, in a frantic attempt to stop us from leaving, but honestly, we weren't safe at the hands of her demise. God only knows what would have happened that summer if we were to have stayed.

The adrenaline was like no other, we managed to escape and slept through the night at a service station. It was cold and dark, I craved the safety that Ireland would knowingly bring to me, a sense of security and sea in between.

It was our great escape, our attempt as a family unit to be together, make memories, and be with the extended family. We made it, we made it to the Emerald Isle and for that I was thankful. I was able to unwind, let my hair down and toast to what felt like my new freedom. Our family was in disbelief of the news, the knowledge that in fact my mother was a monster, unhinged, unwell if you will.

Enough was enough, both my aunties (my mum's sisters) finally called Judgement Day. They contacted social services, informing them of their worry and concern for each of our individual safety and wellbeing. Their investigation commenced, we had multiple meetings separately and collectively.

From their findings they concluded it was either us or her that left the family home. This signified the start of needed change, at last someone was finally listening to us. We were heard.

I disclosed the experiences I had endured as a result of her unstable presence. There are a spectrum of events and behaviours I could write, but this book isn't about painting her in a bad light, just outlining a snippet of her isms.

Thankfully, it was decided she would vacate the family home, our full-time care was to be left solely in Dad's hands, my heart was thrilled with joy. I was over the moon, I naively assumed I wouldn't have to anaesthetise such emotional turmoil with booze going forward. Little did I know I wasn't going to grow out of said 'phase'.

She called us all to the kitchen before she left, she recited a letter she'd previously written, to say I wasn't fazed is an understatement, I just wanted her gone. It was apparent that neither one of my siblings was interested in her final goodbye.

Cracks in our now sheltered family unit began to really show. My brothers' would stay with her from time to time, us girls religiously would with Dad. It would cause friction between us, a divide, she was a wicked woman with the ability to gaslight and manipulate anyone. It was clear she was getting in their heads, worming her ideas and opinions into theirs.

I was reluctant to voice my personal views on the matter, but equally lived in fear that my siblings would experience the full extent of what I did. Being a scapegoat for a narcissist isn't fun and games, it's exhausting, it's debilitating, it's emotional suicide.

The biggest heartache was yet to come, I was just beginning to mourn the loss of my mother, metaphorically that is. My whole internal narrative is, 'if my own mother can't love me, who can?' - I'm still doing the emotional work around this, dissecting it piece by piece as I shed each layer of the onion. Let's just say it involves a lot of inner child work, and that's the real bitch, reverting back to all those years.

Trauma, oh beautiful trauma, how I thought I was done with you? Rewind back to December 1st, 2011, it was a dark and cold morning. Dad was away in Bristol the night prior and thankfully there were no arguments amongst my siblings and me. All five of us had woken up but my sister was feeling unwell, so she decided to stay home from school.

I got ready, Asta our family nanny arrived at the house. Tiarnan greeted me that early morning with 'you look lovely'. I was wearing my horse printed dress and a men's knitted cardigan with penny loafers. To set the scene, we lived in an isolated location, on a main road, the layby opposite and slightly further up to our house, was where we caught the school bus to our secondary school.

I headed to the layby with my photography book to sneak a quick cig, it was paramount that I had my morning nicotine or God knows what mood you'd find me in. Tiarnan had the reflector jacket in his bag, it was a blue Addidas over the shoulder one, and I watched him walk up the grass verge. He looked left and right, and right again, he went to cross and BOOM.

I saw his body fly at least 40 yards to the opposite side of the road, my adrenaline immediately kicked in, I dropped everything and ran like Usain Bolt to jump over his body to prevent the oncoming traffic from hitting him again.

There he was, my poor darling Tiarnan in a mess on the floor, blood pouring out of a number of places, his bodily position mangled. At the same time, I was keeping my eye on the car that hit him, it eventually stopped and the driver got out, running towards my brother's body, he went to touch him and I screamed; you never move a body that's experienced a trauma impact.

My youngest sister arrived outside, she instantly knew something was wrong, I ushered her back into the house to get Asta and a blanket. During this time, I was on the phone to 999, screaming, 'my dad pays your wages, hurry the fuck up!'.

Before I knew it my family was outside, my other sister fell to her knees at the side of Tiarnan. The traffic began to build, people began to come over, and the 999 operator asked me to check his pulse. I scanned the area, shaking and selected someone to do what was requested. I couldn't bring myself to do it, I knew there was no pulse, that my poor baby brother wouldn't wake again.

An off-shift ambulance operator stopped and attended the scene, the Police began to arrive and we were moved to the side away from him. At long last the feckin' Ambulance arrived; I was livid at the delay.

Before I knew it, I was on the phone to Nadene getting directions to Warwick Hospital, I couldn't quite remember the route. Silence, you could have cut it with the knife, the car was filled with this energy that replicated fear and terror. Asta couldn't have been any more emotionally supportive or kind during the whole of this trauma.

We arrived at the hospital, brought to a room where two nurses and my mother were. I asked, 'will my brother breathe again?', no answer, I screamed, 'will he fucking wake up?'; all three shook their heads. I lost it, this rage overwhelmed my body, I couldn't contain the physical pain in my body, and the first thing my mother said to me was, 'here we go Saoirse, you and your dramatics'; just a simple reflection of the woman who bore me into this world.

We were sent to yet another room, unbeknown to us it was next to the Chapel of Rest, and then I heard a loud welp, a scream you can only imagine in a horror film. It was my dad, he arrived at the hospital knowing that Tiarnan had been in an accident but unaware that he died at the scene.

I remember entering that room, his iPod still playing, I asked the nurses, 'can you clean the blood off his face please?', just to be told that it had been and they were the marks from the accident. The pain of losing Tiarnan was next to none, it was soul wrenching, heartbreaking and so much more than I can physically write. I just sat there and listened to his iPod with him, anything to keep the momentum of him being alive, even though he'd never breathe again.

We then headed back to our family home, Granny, Granda and my auntie arrived within hours. Upon our arrival I hit the hard stuff (vodka) straight away. Nothing was worse than a call from his orthodontist, I answered the phone to an appointment reminder, I still can't remember what I said but I informed them he had passed.

There was so much to contemplate, to process, I had just witnessed the death of my brother, my wicked witch of a mother was back in the family home and her path was about to cross with her immediate family from whom she'd estranged herself. The fun and games were just about to begin...

CHAPTER 3

SHIT DOWN SOUTH

"Alcoholism is a well documented pathological reaction to unresolved grief"
David Cook

The Irish flocked in their tribes overseas to see us; it was a family reunion but for a sinister reason. My extended family began to arrive in waves, thank God we had the space to accommodate them all. Our house was a beautiful, big home, isolated in the arse end of nowhere. It was complete with a 'chalet' in the back garden, our area to escape and enjoy drinks and music with friends. Seeing my grandparents was exceptionally hard, how can a grandparent process and cope with the loss of a grandchild? They're still so cut up about it now.

The night of the accident, the day we lost our Tiarnan, we went to our school for a memorial held in his honour. I'll never forget seeing my best friend Laura, she just came over and hugged me. No words were needed, I knew exactly what she was saying, her body language translated that.

School couldn't have been any more supportive, I was overwhelmed by the number of attendees, the majority of it was a blur, I was beside myself with the love we received from everyone.

Catherine Williamson had arrived at our door earlier with chicken thighs and soup, God those chicken pieces were out of this world, it was one way of getting us to eat. Catherine was the mother of Tiarnan's best friend at school, Alice. It was moments like this that I really appreciated, it illustrated the support and fondness everyone had for him.

My heart breaks knowing my parents had to bury their child, no parent should have to do that. Tiarnan was a character, he would go and buy Tesco value chocolate for us girls when it was our time of the month, we'd each synced up (in typical woman fashion). He'd put it under our pillows and announce, 'right it's that time of the month, you have your chocolate so no bullshit'.

He was also a little shit; after he died, we discovered graffiti under the canal bridge by ours, he'd sprayed cocks with 'u suck' before them all over the wall. He used to steal some of our wine at sessions we'd have and blow-up deodorant cans. I often joke that if he was still around Dad would be a grandfather by now!

Pure but not so innocent, we wanted the best send off for our little man, shame that Mother dearest dictated the whole thing.

Talk about drama, the estranged character I reluctantly call Mother, was to see her family for the first time since the shit had really hit the fan. Tensions were high, and it didn't help that pretty much each of us was manic. We wanted Tids to be cremated, but no, he was to be buried and so the list continued. Our wants, wishes and needs were ignored, totally ignored.

During this grief-stricken period, Mother proceeded to take photos of the empty wine bottles in us girls' bedroom (we'd had a session most days for the week previous) and took my bedsheet off to get it tested for seamen. She was delusional to be frank, completely obsessed with seeking some bullshit she'd thought up in her head.

I was so grateful to vodka for getting me through, I was drinking straight from the bottle. The funeral was a blur, cemented in my mind is the imprint of his coffin being lowered into the ground. It was heavily attended, with lots of strange and familiar faces congregating to celebrate the 11 years he had graced us with.

The Month's Mind (a mass in honour of the dead a month after their passing) came; I was pissed in the living room, vodka in sight, arranging Tiarnan's clothes (the items he was wearing on the day of the accident) into the shape of how his body was splayed on the floor. My auntie and granny came in and just hugged me as I whaled. I just wanted to reenact the moment my life flipped a whole 180 degrees.

I wanted to drink that pain away, the whole event needed to be boxed in my eyes. I needed to self-soothe and what better way to do it than with voddy-vodka. Dormant volcano is the term I used to best describe myself, it was the perfect description of me at the time.

As life quickly transcended back to 'normality', I recall being with the girls at a friend's where the drinks were flowing. I flipped, I truly lost it, I can't remember what triggered it but I remember feeling a sense of injustice, that I had lost my brother and they were happy. A resentment to say the least.

In true Sersh fashion I smashed the door off the wall and stormed out, I spoke to a friend who was living in Leamington at the time, I recouped at his that evening. I needed a sense of escape and he was offering that with some wine.

It's interesting how resentment can display so differently in each of us, I've seen sober people so angry it's almost as if they've been on a huge coke session. Physically 'gurnin' with pure rage. Many a time, during my active madness, my anger would really reflect that of my mother's, I would viciously slice anyone apart with my acid tongue.

The last time I had to engage with her (during this period) was at Tiarnan's Inquest. It marked a place where the dirt was dug up, where we heard every fact about that hellish day. It was horrid, truly heartbreaking, as the only witness to the accident, my account was played as a pre-recorded interview.

The driver, now I couldn't tell you his name or what he looks like, but he was present with his immediate family. We were allowed to speak with him after the Inquest, he commented that he could relate to the event as his daughter was hit whilst on her bike, yet she was there standing in front of me. I was incandescent with anger, the copper next to me began to stand that bit closer to me, I knew it was time to cool off otherwise I'd have exploded.

He was never prosecuted, as the forensic evidence deemed he was doing 48mph in a 50. To excite some element of closure, an apology would have been greatly welcomed by us as a family. Such a small gesture was never actioned by him. After taking my brother away from me, I can say I no longer resent him, he has to live with the consequences of that frightful morning every day, and I think that's hell enough.

Drinking.com was the central hub of my life, my biggest obsession and compulsion. Post-mother era, it began to drastically increase, and as it did the Anorexia began to crawl in. If I ran out of wine it was pineapple vodka.

Christ that shit was famous in our ends, it was the vilest spirit I've ever drunk (and there have been many). I've never seen the same bottle again, even after all the off-licenses I've fallen in to. I won't lie I miss that electric feeling, the freedom and... oh wait, I think that's what they call euphoric recall. Oh, to be 16 again, when things were, sometimes, so much easier.

Fast forward a couple of years, and the watering hole began to empty. Mother was receiving her maintenance from my dad, and it was a generous amount. I had just received my car crash compensation; you have to be 18 years old to receive any monies from an Irish Court. Things were quite tight financially at home, Dad was a single parent, providing for us 4 kids, and paying for someone else's rent, food, car, and utilities.

So, the good-natured girl that I am, I lent him some money from my compensation to assist with the day-to-day bills; and I was honoured to be able to do this for him, and it was my way of giving back, especially at this unfair time.

Mother had liked to have the finer things in life, and always liked getting what she wanted.

We had to have the very best of everything, Christ the curtains alone cost an arm and a leg. There was no need for it though, particularly as she would never keep the house, and I was washing walls and polishing furniture weekly to keep the place from going under. She was a very fortunate lady to have a man who provided for her when she never paid maintenance toward us children.

Over time, night clubs would diminish the resentments I had against her, dangerous discos were where I would get lost in euphoria, seeking the love of one, or maybe three guys. One time I got white girl wasted, and got lost in a club in Worcester, I managed to get locked in one of the rooms and began to trip out. The night is a blur, aside from my dad driving all the way to Worcester to calm me down, he left me all wrapped up and chilled.

Dad was my saving grace, no matter the hour or day he always showed up when I'd lose it due to the booze. These were just my standard nights out, an evening filled with drama and conflict of some sort.

CHAPTER 4

FIRST LOVE

"Sometimes we refuse to see how bad something is until it completely destroys us"
Anon

Normally when people mention their ex, they're slagging them off. In this case, I no longer resent him, me or the situation. It very quickly went from love to toxicity to diabolical. People got in the way; they were hurt. How do I fathom a starting point with this, either way the can of worms will be opened!

The darling bloke I thought would forever be by my side, how wrong was I? We were 13, I was sat drinking vodka straight from the bottle, he was ripping a bong in one of our local parks. Loves' young dream. Two kids who were getting up to no good, it was part of growing up right? The thing is we never outgrew that stage, we went on to fall into active addiction as a pair.

There was always something different about him, not just his unique hair, he oozed confidence, mostly ego. Our first date was cancelled by moi, I had to stay at home to be with one of my siblings. I remember being so nervous for the rearranged second one. I wasn't just meeting his parents, between them and his siblings, there was a lot of first introductions.

I arrived; he was at the front door on the phone to the restaurant booking our table. Better late than never I suppose. The initial intros happened, and we headed up to his bedroom. His beer fridge was full of flavoured cider, at the time I wasn't the biggest fan of it, but booze was booze. He'd previously drank the fridge worth's from date numero uno, so they were the replenished stock.

I wasn't really eating at this point and much to my dismay I found out we were heading to a Chinese, The Ruby. He urged me to order, I chose the sweet and sour chicken (he hated it). After a few more drinks, minimal food intake, we headed to the local social club to see the lads. Most of the night is a blur, I was 19 and frequently in black out.

Pissed as a pair of farts we returned to his, I swore to myself I wouldn't be the girl who had sex on the first date, but I began stripping, and before you know it I was on top of him. Until I stopped to throw up outside his bedroom window. My ego inflated as I'd practically taken his virginity (he never finished in a girl before). I declared such a monumental thing in his 'lads' group chat. Sersh the virgin slayer - cringe much.

The best was yet to come, an introduction to my 'borderline personality disorder'. A few weeks later, I had a flare up, I was bemused as to why and how this bloke was interested in me, I was falling hard at this point, and that frightened me. I hit the bottle straight away, I was incapable of processing these emotions, let alone making sense of them.

Drunk texting him, I expressed my desire to push him away, I needed to ensure he'd jump over my hurdles, that he could pass the test. He jumped straight in a taxi and headed straight to mine. No questions asked, just simply came. I cried, we sat up chatting, vulnerable; I sat and voiced my deepest fears.

It began to dissipate the fear, he reassured me, and in typical Sersh fashion I exerted my power and control the best way I knew, through sex. It was still the early days for us, but apparently it was never too early to be love bombed. I'll never forget the moment he uttered those 3 words 'I love you', he was on top, he looked me deeply in the eyes and said, 'I really, really, really, really... LOVE YOU'. Instantaneously, pigs were flying and I felt complete, I think he meant to say 'like you', but for me it was perfect.

For a girl who was desperate for love, I felt as if I had hit the jackpot, I was finally part of the 'loved' crowd. It felt sublime, nothing more than a dream come true. Yes, that's a real reflection of what BPD is like, being unable to process your emotions normally, experiencing extreme highs and lows.

He began to stay at mine and impressively pronounced each of my siblings' names correctly. I'll never forget pulling up on the drive to my dad washing the windows, talk about a first meeting. I don't think I had ever witnessed my dad doing that household chore before. Thankfully all was well and good, the first introduction went as I imagined, it was just fine.

We began to drink together regularly, hiding bottles of Baileys (lol it was only the £3 bottles from Lidl), resorting to my room to secretly devour the lot.

One night we ate some pesto pasta, unbeknown to him, he had a pine nut allergy, before we knew it, his face had swelled up along with his throat. My baby sister prompted us to call an ambulance, they arrived on blues and twos, he was adamant he wouldn't go without a bottle of Baileys, so I lied and said I'd brought it with me.

He was a stubborn mule, wanting to leave hospital ASAP to return to his drinking. His face was expressive when I broke the news that I was not accompanied with a bottle of booze. It took a lot of effort to encourage him to remain admitted to the ward.

In my sheer panic, and being the people pleaser I am, I rang my work frantically to inform them I wouldn't be in, but I never considered that it was 03:00 in the morning - so sorry again Alison. As I fell asleep, unbeknownst to me, he had discharged himself before receiving his allergen test results, and we were in a taxi on route home.

I conveniently assumed that our love story was totally normal, especially in how we both drank. It was the fundamental foundation of our relationship, I was in love, actively drinking and restricting my food intake, my self-will had run riot.

I'll never forget the moment my psychiatrist said I was an alcoholic at 19 years old. I'd just entered my first real relationship, and to have that thrown at me was like a sack of shit, or a led balloon. Plus, I was 19, my life was only beginning now my family shit had finally quietened. How the fuck was I supposed to digest this?

Before you know it, I was shipped off to Bayberry Manor for 28 days of rehabilitation for EDNOS (Eating Disorder Not Specified) and alcoholism. My ego ensured I went in sober, sober to prove a point, that in ACTUAL fact I was not an alky and the bitch was wrong.

The prescribing Doctor didn't know what to do with himself, flustered and confused when I said I hadn't drunk he cast me to one side. I spent the entirety of that stint convincing everyone I was the total opposite of an alcoholic, and in fact just plagued with an eating disorder. Little did I know that I suffered with a subtle, progressive illness and as the years unfolded, it would finally be revealed.

Bayberry introduced me to fellow alkies, and most importantly AA - a 12-step program which continues to give me a daily reprieve from my condition. I remember crying like hell at my first AA meeting, I couldn't fathom such a concept. Like, how stupid was everyone around me? I was fine.

I played the martyr, using others' experiences to exemplify just how opposite my behaviour and relationship with booze was. I would be condescending and arrogant, both moulded by my denial and shame.

I recall a group session with the adjacent cottage members, a disagreement between a housemate and I came to a head. I went the whole 9 miles, referring to him as someone with a silver spoon in his arse. There was a sense of injustice about the comment he remarked about another present addict, so I felt it was right to give him a taste of his own medicine.

I'll never forget his response - 'no wonder your mother wanted to section you'. I was enraged with sheer anger, filled to the brim with resentment towards this total stranger. I was right, he was wrong, simple as. In actual fact, we were both in the wrong.

My eating disorder ran riot during this admission, I was restricting and successfully losing weight. Hell, I even fainted in the bathroom, an ambulance was called, I was ok thankfully. We had our own private chef in the Manor, I would often 'fall' asleep just before meal times and go for long walks across the fields to burn off any digested calories.

Before I knew it, after a few hard-hitting family therapy sessions, I was discharged. I had completed my stay there totally booze-free, whilst engaging with my eating disorder thoughts and behaviours. I was certainly not cured.

At the best of times I don't reciprocate well to change, especially in comparison to a standard person. At that young age, between enduring a 4-week stay in a rehab setting, to then uproot from a home which symbolised such trauma, was a lot to digest.

It was a blessing to have my grandparents assist with the move, I always welcomed any spent time with them. Much to their dismay, my then boyfriend was more concerned with his drinking, rather than helping with our downsize. He had hit the bottle on the day of my discharge, it really illustrated his support for me.

Needless to say, we had successfully moved to Leamington. At long last, I wasn't confined to the arsehole of nowhere - I was in the town I chose to call home. I was no longer isolated or plagued with the death of my brother.

Months later, Hyde Park welcomed their Annual Winter Wonderland, so I and the then boyfriend headed off, I discussed with Dad about having a drink, having ‘stayed off it’ for months. To be frank, I obsessed about it all the time, I’m not 100% sure if I did or didn’t drink during this period, but at long last mulled wine hit my lips, it was a warm blanket on a cold day. I finally got some reprieve from my active disease. I savoured every sip.

My drinking publicly commenced from that moment, no more hiding or lying, I was free to drink as and when I pleased. Before you know it, our love story prevailed, we were the ‘it’ couple, and our adventures around the world started with Paris. Yes, beautiful old Paris for my 20th, it was meant to be a surprise but he spilt the beans accidently.

We visited the Eiffel Tower, River Seine and the Moulin Rouge all in one evening, a black-tie event that both of us made the effort for. Ego aside, the little black dress number I wore caught the attention of many. I had strangers approach me with compliments, some people even stopped in their cars to comment on how beautiful I looked. Christ, I don't think I have ever felt as good as that day.

Turning 20 in the Moulin Rouge was something else, between that and having our own private butler at the hotel, I couldn't have asked for anything else. I even managed to manipulate the night porter into opening the bar for us, he gave us glasses of red wine from Chateaux Monbazillac for nothing. I played the role of a rich, young American (they assumed I was from the States!) who would famously pay them a huge tip upon our departure - they never received this.

I was addicted to playing a role, reflecting various characters that each retracted far away from my authentic self. Little did I know I wasn't to meet the real me until I entered sobriety. The art of holding up the mirror at oneself was yet to come.

I eagerly anticipated my next birthday, but during this time anorexia festered, I was becoming a walking corpse, I was restricting and excessively exercising to the point I was verging on a very unhealthy weight. I continued to hide bottles of alcohol from my partner and my family, I was occasionally drinking and driving, I needed the booze to get some peace from my eating disorder head.

I turned up to my 21st birthday party at The Royal Pug, I have a scrapbook to commemorate the event. It was great, all my nearest and dearest were there, yet I was so distracted by how I looked. Stuck in a state of self-obsession about my body image, I asked Laura if I looked fat, she said, 'I'm not even going to go there'.

Consequently, for my 21st we returned to Paris. I'll never forget my 21st, I woke up surprised that I wasn't showered with gifts, I thought I was just going to work... well it was just another average day in my eyes. Then the news broke, and off to Paris we flew, I had the biggest inclination that my sister (who had been inter-railing around Europe) was waiting in my bedroom. Can I add just how fabulous the Ice Bar/Hotel was, it was magical. And there she was, hidden in the old lavatory, much to my joy and excitement.

We popped around Paris the only way I knew best, via the pubs and bars, or watering holes if you may. I was electric, so full of sheer happiness, albeit I was starving myself at the time. The day after my birthday, we headed to Chanel where I purchased a card holder and a set of earrings. It had been my dream to own something from Chanel on my 21st. I felt like a lady, royalty if you will.

I was inclined to the finer things in life, such as luxury items I could never afford but always dreamt of. It was revealed that my trip to Paris was only for a short period and to be continued in Barcelona. We said goodbye to my sister and commuted on the last leg. Barcelona is one buzzing city, talk about culture, urban delights and hidden treasures. I instantly fell in love.

Still in my bubble, I took everything in, but of course the cherry on top was an argument. Shock, it was a drunken one that concluded with him asleep on a roundabout and me wandering the late-night streets of an unknown city getting groped by a stranger. I couldn't tell you what it was all over, more than likely spilt milk. Our arguments largely took place under the pretence of drink, something two infallible individuals never chose to admit.

It's sad to reflect upon, so sad... our lives centred by drink and drama. I feel sorry for my younger self, to have put myself through such shite. My epicentre was inhabited with the happiness of a liquid drug, but more was yet to come.

CHAPTER 5

ANA, MY OLD FRIEND

"Obsessive control is the darkroom where negatives are developed"

Michael J. Fox

As you found out earlier in my story, I first experienced sexual assault at the tender age of four years old. This was the catalyst for my eating disorder, I began restricting from that point. I mirrored my mother's behaviours with food. The mind is so powerful and impressionable during those developmental years.

You see, I acknowledged my mother being happy when she was eating salad. I remember calling my granny to ask, 'is grass like salad?" She replied, 'yes'. From that day I began hiding my food and eating three strands of grass as a substitute. I was restricting in order to starve the insidious emotion of shame, pain and guilt I held dearly after my experiences with that abusive neighbour.

I continued to emulate her behaviours, binging and restricting, it was a never-ending cycle. The 'Skinny Minnie' was apparent, particularly when my granda was over and he commented on my skeletal frame which protruded through my vest.

He was in shock at how I looked, questioning my eating and whether or not I was at least consuming something. I was in primary school at this point, and it was an elephant in the room I was desperately trying to deflect from.

I carried these behaviours with me through to secondary school. After all, they had proved to be essential in changing how I felt and creating a sense of 'numbness' within my world.

My general experience of school feels like a blur, I never felt like I fitted in, I was never short of friends but lacked a sense of identity. I now know this is a trait of my alcoholism, never fitting in; feeling outcasted; lacking an identity.

School dinners were a luxury I never turned my nose up to, I would compensate for eating said treats by walking excessively around our 1.5-acre field back at the house. I was especially partial to the chocolate cracknel; ham and cheese paninis and white chocolate cookies. They were canteen classics if you ask me.

Equally, I'd find myself emptying my lunch into bins at school so as to set the impression I'd eaten it during the day. Or I would often return home with a lunch box full of pasta, exclaiming it had overheated in the sun, causing it to go off. I was full of excuses as to why my food wasn't eaten; I was becoming good at lying.

One time, when Mother lived with us prior to her grand exit, she accused me of purging in the shower. This was on the basis I decided to have one straight after getting off the school bus. Now to be frank, I did begin purging around the age of 14. It had many benefits for me, it was a way to physically release what I had consumed, whilst ascertaining control over my then turbulent emotions.

That sense of 'lost control' was something I eagerly wanted to fix. Something that needed to be changed internally, and the only way to do so was through restriction and purging. I needed to fix how I felt.

After Mother left, I saw several therapists, all of whom varied in their approach to delivering therapy. The worst experience was a lady I saw privately. She had questioned why I was drinking excessive amounts of water. Wasn't it obvious? I was water loading in turn to falsify my weight and cure my hunger pangs.

I once attended an appointment where she stated that by losing weight, I was making her look bad. I was in complete disbelief that she was more concerned with how it affected her. This threw me, I was being gaslighted by my therapist, so I decided to bring my sister along, in the hope that she'd confirm this was the case.

My sister's initial impression confirmed my suspicions, she wasn't a huge fan of the therapist, so my time with her ended quite abruptly. And rightly so.

It's concerning and difficult to process that, at times, some professionals are fixated more so with the number on the scale, as opposed to the patient in question and their health and wellbeing. I referred to her as my 'Tepid Therapist'.

Over time my behaviours deteriorated and worsened. I became the 'Strolling Sersh', the one who would walk everywhere, but who also favoured the long way around. I was, on average, walking 20+ miles per day, it became my religion, I was obsessed with burning calories. I desired a complete calorific deficit, anything to maintain the continuing decrease to my weight.

I would monitor my weight numerous times a day, being a slave to the scales. I wouldn't allow myself to hydrate until I reached 10 miles of walking. I was consumed, ironically, by this voice in my head that continually reminded me I was fat, worthless and lazy. It was a record on repeat, I would hardly sleep. It's hard to depict whether that was due to the adrenaline from the fight and flight mode, or sheer starvation.

I would walk and exercise even more to compensate for the excessive alcoholic calories I'd drink each day. Some of my individual daily walks would consist of 7-10 miles at a time, and on those I would be accompanied with the presence of vodka or cider. I would hide the booze, smuggling it out of the house, and I'd be off on my jollies. I'd get lost, aimlessly walking in circles, in hope I'd achieve my intention of weight loss. I was desperate to shed the fat.

Cider was my greatest contradiction, it's high in calories yet I drank ample amounts of it. My head would convince me it was like squash, a way to get a hit of booze without getting too obliterated. I needed to reframe from becoming too intoxicated, I needed to maintain control.

I used to hide bottles of it in my room, assuming this was normal behaviour for an anorexic like me. I would ensure my stock was always replenished with said bottles, whilst accompanied with sweets and treats. I would happily hoard my feared foods, I would have all sorts hidden, from chocolates to crisps.

Encompassed with fear, I would often find myself selecting one of these feared items, shakingly opening the packaging all to be greeted with the sweet smell of chocolate I craved so deeply. I never had the balls to proceed with the ritual of eating the bar, it was too painful. It would go straight in the bin.

I was lost, unable to identify reality from the mental scenarios running through my head. I was obsessed with food, exercise and drink. I tolerated people only if I'd completed my exercise for the day, restricted accordingly and drunk to drown out the voices in my head.

Things were spiralling out of control, I was becoming a shell, I chose to exist rather than to live. This led me, eventually and thankfully, to the woman who I believe was God sent, Miriam my therapist.

She could see straight through my bullshit; she provided me with the insight to understand and face up to just how unwell I actually was.

I never realised how good a liar I'd become and how rife my eating disorder was. I'd achieved a bulimic's dream, I didn't need to put my hands down my throat to purge, it would just come up. I lied about what and how much I ate at every meal.

Miriam introduced me to effective meal plans, eating 3 meals and 3 snacks per day. I tried my best to adhere to this but it was too painful and challenging. One time, she got me to draw an outline of what I perceived to be my silhouette, it hugely differed from the reality, my waist was the length of her hand.

I started to realise that I couldn't go on the way I was, that I was slowly dying. I was becoming sick and tired of being sick and tired. I knew something had to change, and thank God, it eventually did.

I visited the GP with my dad...

At the tender age of 21, I didn't realise how sick my 'double A's' (anorexia and alcoholism) had made me. From that first meeting with my GP, I was immediately referred to the local Eating Disorder Services.

I'll never forget the build up to that initial consultation, I was so nervous, riddled with fear they'd laugh at how fat I was. I pleaded with my dad to leave, as the appointment became more and more delayed, begging him to go. Then the consultant called me in, they discussed my symptoms, behaviours and thoughts. I was waiting for a suggested diet, one to aid further weight loss at a quicker rate because I knew, I knew they were going to say my weight was off the Richter scale.

How wrong could I have been, how poorly was I back then? So poorly that I had to be admitted as an urgent case to a facility in the Cotswolds.

It differed from my first experience of rehab; this time I was going in to put something in me as opposed to putting something down. Well, I guess you could say put something down the hatch. I remember not even drinking a sip of water before my admission, arriving at the hospital with my partner, my siblings and Pops. Everything was coded, the doors, the lifts and rooms were locked. I was oblivious to the fact this would be my home for 9 whole months - I'd never been to the Cotswolds prior to this.

Christ, where do I start when dissecting this chapter of my life? I wanted to get better because my man loved me, he loved me at my mentally and physically lowest, so there must have been some good in me, right? Saying goodbye to my family and him was heartbreaking, I was unaware of what I'd signed up for, a daily routine that took me some time to adhere to.

I had to eat 6 times a day, that's 3 meals and 3 snacks a day, all of which were time limited. I was greeted with half a jacket potato with beans and cheese. I remember sobbing as I painfully took each mouthful, because that was the aim of the game, get better and get OUT.

I felt a huge disconnect from my family in those initial first few days, none of them had contacted me - poor me, why me? I was on the pity pot, the whole world had to revolve around me, everything in my life had become small, and no I'm not just referring to my physical state. I was hurt that I hadn't heard from them though.

I was an anorexic who ate less than 500 calories a day and exercised her legs for a minimum of 30+ miles per day. I was a chronic case allegedly, much to my dismay. I was in pure denial about my ego, the self-obsession and illness that plagued my waking and sleeping thoughts.

I'm reluctant to say I was a codependent case, my relationship with my partner oozed it. He tolerated a lot, he tolerated my panic attacks, and those weren't pretty. I would almost fit and seizure like an epileptic, unable to control the surge of anxiety and fear that dictated my physical being. Hats off to him he was able to manage these and guide me through them.

I found comfort in writing, in physically signing away my current state of feeling. It gave me solace as I independently learnt to live by myself with a bunch of other sick patients. It was hard to make my way around others' eating habits, and behaviours such as hiding food, over exercising, and purging. We were a group of competitive kids all wanting to fight against the grain of getting better, a ripple effect. It was hard to compete with people I saw as much sicker than myself, but my greatest competition was me.

I would long for my man during the difficult times, I joked with him that I wouldn't need to see him for at least a week, but by day 2 he had visited. He made me feel that we were invincible together. Initially I wasn't allowed out for even a cigarette, I was on the old nicotine replacement things, so to make things exciting we would have sex in the family and meeting room.

My non-existent libido came out to play because what else was there to do? Fuck all. Plus, it was another outlet for burning calories. Back then I would even swallow, I was that much of a catch, I would swallow the 70 calories in his cum because I was a fucking rock star. That was a major ‘FU’ to anorexia, painfully swallowing those extra calories all in the name of love.

One time we were in the boardroom (where ward rounds happened with the Consultants Team). It got saucy, and jeez did I cum all over the chair. It was also a massive FU to the medical team; they were denying me of my behaviours and formed habits. They were breaking my rituals which caused my rebellious and defiant side to come out.

Within a matter of weeks of my admission, I was awarded my first galivant off the unit. I was granted a trip in the car; I wasn’t allowed to exert any unnecessary energy; a deemed ruling from the ‘Gods who must be obeyed’. Yeah, it took me a while to warm up to my consultants and the ward team.

I was greeted by Dad who had some smokes for me, Christ the relief I had from that first puff. I obviously couldn't ask for booze; I knew he wouldn't bring that. It was a pleasure to be in his company, after all he was and is my greatest supporter.

I'll never forget the nurse who admitted me, she asked if I was alcohol dependent, a question I always answered "no" to. I wanted to say yes, I was desperate for some sort of hit, but anorexia was stronger and more prevalent than the alcoholism at that time.

I found it incredibly hard, frustrating at the very least. As I sit here and conjure up those old, boxed away memories I feel a sadness and grief for that lifeless girl. I'm the heaviest I've ever been as I write this, all with thanks to my new medication regime. Honestly, it's something I find so painful to accept, adjusting to my new size and shape is excruciating, and worlds apart from my previous silhouette. Yet, acceptance is the key, and I need to hold on to an 'attitude of gratitude' for being healthy, much to my dismay!

Darling Ana, as I now call my anorexia, still lingers, just as much as my subtle alcoholism. There's no running from the bastard pair.

A swig of chai latte and I'm back in the room, back in my bedroom in the unit. It was the largest room on the top floor which benefited an over-exerciser like me. I used to work out in my ensuite but only once I was awarded bathroom privacy. That's right, I wasn't allowed to piss in peace through fear of collapsing, self-harm, purging or exercising.

All I wanted was to shit, I hadn't been in over a month, 12 laxatives deep (on a daily basis) and still nothing moved until Lactulose was introduced. That was my saving grace, the pain was incomprehensible. Allegedly, my consultant used to give patients bubbles to blow on the toilet, it would help release and ease them of flatulence issues (TRY IT if you get stuck!).

To pass time, I filled the pages of countless notebooks with daily entries, an implosion of my thoughts and feelings. I was able to measure my progress, using these as reference points. Idiotically, I decided a few years ago, that it was it was time to part with them. I'm not sure what came over me, quite possibly I felt it was a way to free myself from darling 'Ana'.

Although, I have kept some of the letters and cards newly made inpatient friends and family sent me. Since I was heavily restricted by the activity I could do, I accumulated a lot of spare time, so I followed the crowd and began to create a scrapbook. It was a way to document every monumental moment in my recovery journey.

You'd find a mixture of reference points such like my PMOs (post meal observations) being reduced to 30 minutes; the first chocolate bar I'd eaten in years; my first snack out of the unit. These were instrumental in my recovery, a way to evidence to the medical team that I was getting better.

At the beginning of my admission, I was successfully adhering to a continuous completion rate of my meals and snacks, I thought I had it sussed but the bitch in my head soon riled up.

One of the support workers pre-warned me that it wouldn't be plain sailing, and my God was she right. I began to spiral, losing my shit because I was being made to eat and denied the sweet relief of a cigarette; I was classed as too poorly to go out the front for one. I threw my toys out of the pram one evening when our medication had been delayed, all I wanted was my nicotine, just a crutch and substitute for the booze.

As time went on, I was awarded certain privileges like smoking, this worked to my benefit, I was able to dispose of food I had hidden in my big boot like slippers. I hid half a bloody baguette in my slipper one time, how insane was I! I'd take advantage of my new found freedom by purging in the street, as well as discarding any food I'd snook into my clothing. I would have locked me up if I'd seen me! And these are just a fraction of the insane things I would do.

One night I spoke with my sister on the phone, I came clean about hiding food and not being 100% honest about the amount I was still exercising. She wasn't surprised by this at all, but what surprised me was that I had a moment of clarity as I spoke with her, a desire to be transparent and accountable (for a change).

From that point my journey was bumpy, but I gave it my all. There was no time like the present. My freedom was to extend to walks off the unit. I was managing to do nearly 6 miles in just under an hour around the village. One time I showed my peer group the route. On the occasion I did, we were out for longer than allowed, and the nurse came in the minibus for us... we were in the shit, I was the ring leader and held accountable.

Even so, us girls became close; we started going out together for snacks; trips to the cinema and places such as the petting zoo. Time restored the medical team's faith in me, and before I knew it I was allowed to venture into the village for a haircut, or to volunteer in a local charity shop. It was all about integrating back into the community and normal living.

The one thing I worked hard towards was Christmas home leave, I wanted nothing more than to be at home with my then partner and my family. From memory I was given 2 nights leave, and this was my first overnight stay since my admission. I felt sick with anxiety, filled with pure panic at the thought of being responsible for my food and exercise intake. It presented as my greatest opportunity to lose weight without the overbearing supervision of the staff on the unit.

Christmas welcomed the gift of a Tiffany's eternity ring from my man, thank God it wasn't a proposal. I don't believe in them being around big dates and or anniversaries (bad karma that). Little did I know our love wasn't for eternity, it had just embarked on another slippery slope, one I was oblivious to for some years.

My first trip out in Broadway was with him, we pottered around the idyllic Cotswold village, and ended up at the pub, in true Sersh and him style. I had a cider, my first sip led to the initial thought of the next drink, how; when; where was I going to get it?

At the next weigh-in I lost weight, this was the evidence my brain needed (more like craved). It confirmed I could drink alcoholically without detrimental repercussions to the number on the scale. Only as long as I continued to compensate with exercise and food restriction. A right result if you ask me.

I forgot to mention the 5am starts we'd have once a week for weigh in. We were randomly woken at stupid o'clock to minimise our chances of water loading (falsifying our weight).

Throughout my whole admission, I was blessed to have friends visit me, those moments kept my fight alive. I can only assume it was slightly surreal for them, coming to a secure unit, between the key coded rooms and staff checking up on you. It was so kind of them, and as I got better, I gained more entitlements to venture into the village with them or see them whilst I was on home leave.

During my admission, a then friend's dad died unexpectedly. At the time, I wasn't allowed to drive due to my low weight, so I'd commute back home to Leamington on the bus. I was granted leave for the funeral, I remember going to it, and drinking until my heart was content.

Accompanied by my then partner, I felt hugely overwhelmed with dread at the prospect of ever losing my dad. The pain would be unimaginable. My pops means more to me than I can physically articulate.

I returned back to the unit early doors; Dad dropped me back on his way into the Bristol office. Still pissed I managed to woof down my breakfast to sober me the fuck up. I must have smelt like a brewery.

My drinking continued to excel; it gave me some relief from the anorexic mindset I was all too familiar with. I started to sneak booze into the unit, vodka was a companion I would smuggle in with me. I was successful every time, it just smothered the thoughts, drowning them out one sip at a time.

A total of 9 months later, 'Freedom Day' was ahead of me, I was finally set to be discharged from Huntercombe Cotswold Spa. I couldn't believe my eyes, the scrapbook I documented my snacks; day trips out; and allowances in was filled by patients with their best wishes. It filled me with joy and gratitude.

I also felt a lot of fear, fear for my rehabilitation back into the community, and being discharged to my local Eating Disorder Services. It was time to do this on my own, to step back into reality, one crumb at a time.

CHAPTER 6

CHRISTMAS TREE AND A 20 BAG

"The thought of suicide is a great consolation: by means of it, one gets through many a dark night"

Friedrich Nietzsche

I've been contemplating this chapter for a while now, putting it off because of the pain which ultimately resurfaces. This marks a pinnacle in my drinking career, my eating disorder was contained thank God. I'm listening to Taylor Swift, her Folklore and Evermore albums got me through my breakup with my then partner who had so enabled my habitual self-abuse, this chapter marks the beginning of the end.

Memories flood back to this time of my life; I was so naive and optimistic for my future. Sure, who wouldn't be, I'd just kicked anorexia's arse, I was nearly weight restored after a gruelling 9 months of rehabilitation. Hats off to the NHS for saving my life and investing in a girl who desperately needed help. I'm one of the fortunate ones, and eternally grateful.

During the last few months of my stay at the clinic, my leaves were extended which gave me ample time to spend refamiliarising myself with home. I accidentally stumbled upon a new build development about a mile from town and without hesitation I visited the sales office. I was sold, sold at the thought of my then partner and I starting our new chapter with a mortgage, we were both committed to each other so naturally this was the next step.

My dad was in disbelief at this idea of mine, but I was determined to make it a reality, I had all the will in the world. So, in true Sersh fashion I kick started the process, assigned a mortgage advisor and hey presto we were off.

Halloween marked the day we got our keys; our combined hard work had paid off. I couldn't contain my excitement. The carpets weren't being fitted for a couple of days, but we had a mattress and that's all that mattered. Our first home, being my usual anal self, I wanted to decorate and get things sorted.

Molly came over with a mop bucket full of cleaning goodies (that's the way to my heart!), she was one of the first people to visit us at Soans Drive. She's one of my favourites, best gals if you will, I would be lost without her love, support and most importantly her forgiveness.

That first Christmas, to commemorate the 'Fizz Festivities', we met with Molly and her partner at a local pub. We had a blast as always, and boy were the drinks flowing. Any normal person would have a few at the pub and call it a day, but no I had some before and after our time with them. Him and I still hadn't bought a Christmas tree, so fuelled by our mixed inhibitions we thought it was a good idea to steal one of the pub's.

Yep, that night ended with us smuggling a 2-foot Christmas tree from a pub - the great incentive was it came with battery powered lights and pegs. I attached chocolates and sweets to the pegs for my then fella, so he'd have a homemade advent calendar. I was so desperate for everything to be perfect.

Before we knew it, we were mixing business with pleasure, I began working alongside him at a local cafe he managed. It was ironic, a recovering anorexic who was yet to discover she was an alcoholic, was working at an eatery.

I'm an extremely organised person, and even back then, honest to a degree. The day we got the keys for the house I informed the Benefits Office of the change in my living situation; this automatically closed my account with them. The pressure was on to find work, and there's no Bonnie without Clyde. It was ideal, we would live and work together, perfect for a couple who were utterly obsessed with each other. A recipe for disaster more like.

From drinking on shift to heading to the pub after work, we formed a drinking culture everyone wanted to be part of. No one batted an eyelid, my drinking was hidden in plain sight as I immersed myself within a drinking group, who either drank like me or simply didn't give a toss.

To keep the passion and fire alive, I would occasionally have sex with him at work. There was a close call with one of our colleagues, they nearly walked in on me giving him oral sex, now that could have been awkward. I needed to be desired, I needed to assert power and control, and the best way I knew how was through sex.

The apple cart was yet to be shaken by 'Business 2.0' swiftly taking off and transforming our home into what felt like Waterloo Station. My spare room sadly never made it as a walk-in wardrobe, it was occupied by tarantulas and a burmese albino python. Yep, you read that correctly, you may as well have stepped into Narnia, or your local zoo.

My then partner was fascinated with, and rather talented at breeding the 8-legged things, and so to support him in his endeavours I consented to them living rent free in the house. I can safely confirm I no longer have a fear of spiders, my fear of snakes still remains - when I finally left it was nearing 11+ feet!

Our new found freedom gave me a sense of euphoria, a feeling I kept chasing with each drink and bit of exercise I could squeeze in. I was still counting calories, that obsession was strong, it hadn't left me yet.

We collectively welcomed a 'one in, one out' door policy on the day my ex decided to start selling bud from our home. It was a way to accumulate additional funds to eradicate his debts, at least I thought so. In the end, it transpired it was largely used to a fund his cocaine habits.

A constant supply of drugs and money meant one thing - PARTAYS! It wasn't just a weekend event, somehow our weeknights were booze filled, hosting parties or at our local watering holes. We transformed into the hosts with the most, every Tom, Dick and Harry popped over for illicit drugs and drink.

Pablo Escobar (for the uninformed - cocaine) was a frequent visitor, for years I initially declined it, I was better than any drug takers, I was too superior for that shit. It was as if we were the local Great Gatsby, we were accumulating a wider group of what I know now were acquaintances, former drinking goers.

The high life was ours, and so to celebrate we jetted off to Majorca. It was my first experience of an all-inclusive hotel, and it didn't disappoint, from alcohol slushies to shots, it was an alcoholic's wet dream. Things turned ugly on our second last night, he was in blackout, the Jekyll and Hyde began to creep out.

Challenging and abusive communication from him alarmed the staff, the angry nature of his words wasn't just noticed by my ears. A staff member approached me and said if things were to escalate to call a specific number on the internal phone, stating a certain phrase, which would inform them that things had taken a turn for the worse.

We went back to the room, and BOOM, the dormant volcano exploded. He threw me across the room, smashed the room up, I felt backed into a corner, petrified I called the number. There was a knock at the door, I opened it to armed guards bordering the door frame.

He began to cry, I was asked what I wanted to do, all I remember thinking was 'he'd learn his lesson this time' and never do it again. They took him away, whilst I went to the hospital to be examined. I returned to the hotel, distraught and perplexed by what had happened.

The following morning, I had to borrow money off my padre to pay for a cab to the courts. It wasn't until months later that he discovered the reason why.

I waited eagerly outside for my then boyfriend to emerge; we spoke and I naively thought everything would change for the better.

He never incurred costs from the hotel, the hotel manager kindly let these slip under the circumstances. We managed to get our prints from the photographer, they reflected a happy couple, oh what keeping up appearances can do. I was projecting the learnt behaviours from my mother, as long as all looked well on the outside it didn't matter if you were drowning, appearances were key.

I felt indebted to my then boyfriend, it was as if I owed him the world for putting him in prison in Majorca. We still continued to drink together, that's why our next trip to Greece was so important. It was an essential test to prove we were a power couple, not one who argued violently.

We planned that getaway to Greece with another couple, this was our chance, I was holding on to every last bit, willing for it to go well. Gosh, it sure did, it was the other couple who argued over dinner, I felt for my best friend, she didn't deserve that. In Sersh style I joined her down at the beach, accompanied by booze (knowing she wouldn't drink the cans, so there was more for me) and skinny dipped.

I felt like seeing my tits and 'foof' couldn't make her feel any worse, she cried and we laughed together. In that moment, it was special. Even drunk I was empathetic, and to an extent, I was able to be there for someone other than myself. Upon returning back to the lads, my ex assumed I had run off with his inhaler, but that was the height of our arguing for that short, sunny spell.

To English soil we returned, and our drinking and cocaine sprees reignited, back to a fully operating service. It was business as usual. I must mention that my then man only allowed me to do cocaine with him, never alone or with friends. It was his way of asserting an element of control over me.

I remember the first time doing it, the buzz I got, gosh it was heaven. It accelerated my drinking; I could drink even more than my usual copious amounts whilst on the 'liffer'. One evening, just an average evening may I add, us + booze + cocaine = spontaneity. As we began to watch porn, I shared that I was always bi-curious, desperate to have a good old-fashioned shag with a woman.

Before I knew it we were ordering a hooker to the house, £200 per hour to see your then boyfriend shag another woman, whilst performing a scissor sister act felt like a good deal? He was paying for the coke, and all this supported one of my greatest character defects - self-seeking behaviour.

I was ready for it, I'd fantasise from time to time about having sex with women, so now was the moment to make it a reality. She arrived, I was dressed up in lingerie, we had the drinks flowing, the cocaine on tap. This was the first of many hook-ups, at times we would have 3-4 women and 'mates' join us too.

It's insane to think I'd watch a woman sleep with my then boyfriend, whilst she pleasured me. One woman lap danced our 'mate' and my then man in front of me, I didn't even bat an eyelid. I had this sexual desire that was catalysed by cocaine. It really brought out my dark side.

One time, one of our regulars arrived, it was just my then man and me. She had previously left me a sex toy; it almost signified a trophy. You see, some of those women had allegedly never been down on a female before, I was their first - I was top of the class and happily accepted my trophy.

Christ, I feel sick writing about it, I can't fathom this side of me, I was ruthless, a sexual deviant. Anyway, when my favourite regular arrived, we had one of the best threesomes of my life, it was erotic, I was utterly pleasured, but of course I didn't take notice of any contraception.

For weeks I had all the obvious signs of being pregnant, the sore enlarged boobs, I was eating chocolate, something I never really did after leaving Cotswold Spa. My friend prompted me to get a test, I just ignored her concern.

Then one evening, a few (plenty of) drinks down, I did a test and fuck me, both lines appeared. I sprinted to the shops across the road, screaming at the pharmacists, 'can you get a false positive?' I demanded two of their most expensive tests and ran home. Those poor ladies were left pretty perplexed by this wild woman's behaviour.

Those two tests didn't let me down, they both confirmed my worst nightmare. My initial thought was, 'I'm not stopping drinking' - we went to the pub. We told two of our 'friends' who had promptly met us at the pub.

In my not so sober mental state, I decided to call my then boss to inform her I was pregnant. Why the fuck I felt this desire to share the news, as if I'd just broken my toe, is beyond me.

For a second, I had a bit of clarity, I decided to have a private scan to determine how far on I was. I needed to know if it had a heartbeat, yet we were faced with some challenges. I was referred to the Early Pregnancy Unit as the private clinic couldn't find the bambino. I was poked and prodded, informed I may be having an ectopic pregnancy or a missed miscarriage. The whole time I just obsessed about booze, how could I bring something into this world of chaos I had created?

I wasn't prepared to give it up, and I think deep down I knew he and I weren't ready for parenthood. Isn't it just insane, gifted by the grace of God with a baby, and my addiction was more important. That's the power of alcoholism.

We settled on an abortion; my sister very kindly drove us to the clinic. I decided to have the vacuum method as I didn't have a definitive date of conception. I thought it would be thorough and straight forward, but it was agonising.

Part of the process includes a scan, and I heartbreakingly asked to hear the heartbeat. There on the screen was a part of me and him, a living thing, and I was about to part with it. But I knew in my heavy heart that it was the right thing to do.

For the next year, I suffered from extreme bleeding and infections, it was one thing after another. I was exhausted, but it was ok, I had my drink. I recall being in a pub with my dad prior to the abortion, there I was drinking a pint of beer, he asked if I should, my response was, 'well it's going to die anyway'.

Self-centredness that's what it was, I was so consumed with self I didn't care. My head belonged to the compulsion and obsession of drink; food was substituted with it. I needed to somehow fill the hole in my soul, and thankfully Lottie, my darling black and tan sausage dog provided me with comfort.

She was the best money I had ever spent, all £300 of it, I utterly and unconditionally love her, she is my shadow, a sidekick and has seen me through all the experiences I have and continue to share in this book. I found solace in having something to care for other than myself, but let's be honest I wasn't really doing a great job of that.

A dog can never replace a child, but for me it eased the pain. I'm so desperate to have a family, and it scares me that it may have been my only opportunity. I know though, that my Higher Power has a plan for me, and God will grace me with a child if and when the time is right.

I felt shame and remorse for my actions, but how on earth could I explain to my child 'you were conceived in a threesome with plenty of liquor flowing and cocaine sniffing!'. I'm also a big advocate for mental health, I suffer with Borderline Personality Disorder; a Panic Disorder; Anxiety and Depression just to top it off.

Before my pregnancy, I was in a complex state, I couldn't fathom being weight-restored, the eating disorder thoughts haunted me. I drank to numb them out, to quieten that anorexic head of mine. I was broken with it, I longed for some type of peace of mind. My options were running out, and it left me with only one, that was to commit suicide.

He was downstairs, I was upstairs, I managed to take a shit load of pills, a concoction if you will, all washed down with booze. I vaguely remember seeing a photo of my brother Tiarnan and shouting my then man's name. What had I done? I still don't know if I regret that act of desperation.

He immediately called 999, the ambulance arrived and said that I'd be fine, that I probably was putting it on. For safe measure they brought me in. I don't remember any of this. Laura arrived at the house, she was going to greet me with a birthday present, he explained what had happened and she shot to the hospital.

To have a friend, no, a sister like Laura is something I'm eternally grateful for, she's been my longest standing friend for over 15 years! I was out for the count when she arrived at the hospital, and from what I've been told, it wasn't great.

I quickly deteriorated, Laura was asked to contact my family, she called her fella and got him to bring mine to the hospital. They sat in sheer silence in the waiting room, whilst I was being resuscitated. It wasn't a joke, it was serious. I had nearly crossed that finishing line forever.

I was transferred over to Castle Ward for a few days, I had visitors and my then fella was allowed stay the whole time. It wasn't my first encounter with the crisis team though, I downplayed the fact I truly wanted to kill myself, that I generally didn't see a way out of life. I was done existing; it was time to pull the plug.

I've had several attempts since then, most of which have led me to hospital - but it just wasn't meant to be. As I sit here and write this, it does make me grateful, grateful that I wasn't successful in my attempts. It doesn't stop the suicidal idealisation, but today I have a toolbox for it, I've learnt about the power of talking, sharing where I'm at.

This leads me to loss of a dear friend 5 years ago, darling Grace. Grace and I met whilst I was at Huntercombe, I immediately didn't like her, I'm not sure why, but as time went on, she became like a little sister. Grace was a force to be reckoned with, she was beautiful inside and out.

We would often write to each other; I still have each of her handmade cards. I could always tell it was a card from her by the distinctive neat handwriting. As and when I'm struggling with eating disorder voices, I refer back to them, they give me strength and shed some perspective on the situation.

Like me, Grace had made several attempts on her life until the day came when she was successful in her efforts. She threw herself in front of a lorry, and that was the day so many hearts were shattered. I was informed through social media and instantly threw up. I was due to see her only a couple of weeks later, and the girl owed me a gin and tonic.

She met me once in Birmingham, we got pissed and pretended we were sisters as we mooched through designers such as Louis Vuitton. We had the best of times, and she came back to mine, we smoked a bit of pot, although my then bloke insisted she didn't. He kindly reminded her not to drink like for like with me, and in her intoxicated state we begun making beans which she started eating cold from the saucepan.

Within a matter of time, she was then sick all over my sofa, we mopped her up and got her comfy, and the following day said our goodbyes after a lush brunch at a cafe. It was just one of the many good times we had with each other, we were both free, both trying to navigate life whilst recovering from anorexia.

The moment I learnt of her passing haunts me, it breaks my heart to see the world lose someone with such potential; potential to effect change in a broken system. The funeral couldn't have been any more of a credit to her and her family, it was beautiful. Losing Grace was a stark reminder of the insidious pain eating disorders and mental health issues can bring.

All I can do is advocate talking, sharing an experience with someone who similarly understands takes the power of it out. And writing, write it down, like I'm doing.

CHAPTER 7

ROCK 'N ROLL THROUGH THE NIGHT

"Drugs are a waste of time. They destroy your memory and your self-respect and everything that goes along with your self-esteem. They're no good at all"

Kurt Cobain

Between ‘Ladies of the Night’ and “Pablo Escobar’s Finest’ life was one rock ‘n roll show, one I was orchestrating. You see I’d manipulate everyone around me, I’d be a chameleon with plenty of drinking friends from different groups. This was intentionally planned so their paths would never cross, minimising their chances of ever conversing about my long list of fuck ups, past and or present.

I started to fall in love with other drugs such as MDMA and pills, I would reach states of euphoria I never thought imaginable. The best way to complement the experience was by attending raves with friends. We would hit up Passion in Coalville, it was a blast and my best friend would be whoever offered me a chewing gum. I would drink and drink on the drugs, whilst many were impartial.

Ha, in the early hours of the morning after the rave had finished, we went back to our hotel, I thought it would be a fun idea to drop a pill and hit the hay. My then boyfriend, the current 'best friend' and I woke up in a bed full of piss, yep it was soaked through, God bless the cleaners.

The worst was the 25th anniversary, I'd just dropped a pill, and all of a sudden, I was tripping... I see two paramedics run past me, I turned to my ex confused, but in fact I was seeing things clearly. A chap had sadly died on site after over-indulging in some form of drugs. The rave was cut short and we were each escorted out. He was the first person to die at one of their events.

Although I was shaken up, it didn't knock any sense in to me. I was still happy to take my drugs at home, or any social event. I would hide them in period pads as bouncers would never dare go near them, it was my 'trick of the trade'.

I jumped continually from euphoria to anger to euphoria again. An emotional rollercoaster that saw me, whilst in the intoxicating midst of the abortion, throw myself down the stairs, screaming in front of my impregnator's friends, "you made me kill this baby!". I didn't want to exist for that moment in time, I wanted to expel any feeling or thought. I knew there was a high chance I would have killed the baby, what with the copious amounts of booze I was digesting. Yet, I so desperately wanted to reunite with that part of me that I'd lost.

To paint me in another beautiful light, I once ripped the TV off the wall, I was in an angry rage, a pure Jekyll and Hyde. It was as if I was Scrappy Doo in the flesh; little, but ready to physically take anything on. Of course, I ensured I had an audience to perform in front of - that way, I could focus on the ripple effect of my actions and feed the guilt/shame cycle I used to excuse my drinking and drug habits.

Without smoke there's no fire, and boy did my actions reap a reaction, never a response - this is something I have learnt to do overtime; pause, respond as opposed to react. He would retaliate largely by smashing his phone, he went through physical moments also, but they're for another day. Or the house would be the target for his tyrannic outbursts, one item of furniture, one wall decorated with a hole at a time.

As things spiralled so did my lies, an insidious web of lies to protect the truth I didn't want exposed. It was our friend's first night out as parents, they came to ours to have a few bevvies (it was never a few for me) and to chill the fuck out. My ex went on about his suicidal idealisations, and this automatically highlighted a red flag for me, it only led down the Pablo Escobar road - and he'd promised that he wouldn't do it again.

Taking a step back I totally appreciate the empty promises of "I'll never do it again" - I would constantly obsess over not drinking, or what soft drink (wine, cider or beer) I'd have instead of vodka. I would ruminate about how, when, where and why I'd end up drinking even after fighting with myself profusely, I had no fight in me anymore, that ship had sailed.

Back to that evening, I lost it, the dormant volcano had erupted, as our friends left I screamed, "I cheated on you". That statement was a lie, I was actually raped by a stranger during the time we were on a break. I was broken, everything from my childhood flooded back, it came in tsunami waves, it resurrected that little girl who couldn't scream loud enough, desperate to be heard.

Yes, it's very Ross and Rachel in a twisted sense. I thought it would be okay to write about it, I thought I'd addressed the incident but right now it's something I can't be transparent about. It was a horrid incident; one which will remain private for the time being.

In the midst of it all, I got up and left, my Louis Vuitton in one hand full of booze, the dog in the other. Straight off to Annabelle's I went, barely shoed and clothed but with all the essentials including nicotine. Annabelle is my soul sister, the woman I lived with for a long period of time during the aftermath of this shit show. She's the bean to my seahorse in paradise - only she will understand that!

My ex lost it with me, but all I could do was cower after dropping such a bombshell. I hit the bottle, I bottled it all up, playing lip service to those around me. Trying to figure out how to untangle the truth, he was the first person I disclosed the honest truth to.

Again, we found ourselves on a break, it was the end of many as per usual, it went on like swings and roundabouts. In this time, I reconnected with a flame from the past, I needed my ego stroked. A distraction if you will, and as always, I magnetised toward someone with an equal interest in drugs and booze like me.

This particular person emulated my obsession for booze, he became infatuated with me, I was his 'baby' he over-indulged me in compliments, he was everywhere I looked. He'd even memorised my car's registration plate.

I would smoke weed with him, drink excessive amounts and sniff like it was going out of fashion. I really made it snow one Christmas Day, the first thing I done upon waking up was drill a line, washing it down with a bottle of beer. I got my sister to collect me on route to the family house, and of course I created a fiasco, it was all about me, I was chasing that first line. My mind was utterly focused on getting the beers in, instead of spending quality time with my family over the festive period.

Before I knew it, my clean time from the ex was soon to be broken, I relapsed in love that

January. I tried to commit suicide again after a rough comedown from the copious amounts of cocaine I'd endured. All I wanted was my ex, and by God did he come running. He arrived at the hospital and just held me, held me tightly, I felt safe, like nothing was an issue. I ensured my other 'acquaintance' was kept at arm's length and didn't visit me, he cried as I explained what I'd tried to do.

I was constantly running in fear, fear from myself and emotions, I desperately sought out oblivion, but that stopped working, and my only option was to give up and wave the white flag.

I'll never forget that morning in January, the 'acquaintance' turned up at my door, questioning why I was back at my house with my ex. I said his nan had taken ill, as his cum trickled down my leg. We had literally just had sex, it was electric, I never saw myself as a cheater until that day. I couldn't believe I'd ran straight back to my safe place.

But it wasn't all roses for this lady, over time I lost it, I was unstable. I turned up at our house, I tore the place to shreds, smashing every item in sight. I was a bull with a red flag, and my ex had called his dad who began to video record me upon his arrival... I had finally, really lost it, I ensured he captured me saying, "I don't consent to this recording". All I wanted was my home back, it felt like such an injustice, my ex living there whilst I was living with Belle, I hated knowing it was used for parties with prostitutes.

On one occasion, a good few bottles of Prosecco later, I had smashed the place up, throwing his weed gummy bears out of the window, screaming, "he's a drug dealer". Someone had called the police, my dad arrived as they did, I had to answer some domestic questions - all my ego could fixate on was that I was pulling the wool over their eyes, they had no idea I was intoxicated.

It concluded with me leaving the property, driving away under the influence with the police none the wiser. I went home and continued drinking.

Those incidents didn't tear us apart however, we still circled in and out of each other's lives for quite some time. Snapchat reveals all, I coerced him into getting black-out drunk to the point he passed out so I could access his phone. Thanks to my mass manipulation my worst fear was confirmed - he had been messaging his ex.

And hell was I going to stand for that! I messaged her 'God knows what', causing her to let loose on me via the social media platform. I called her parents 'alcoholics'; talk about irony, something I'm not proud of either. I am sorry to that girl and her family for prying on their personal lives. Belle was there when she went ape on the phone, the girl had found out where I lived, and there was me thinking I was crazy!

I needed to confirm the fact that I was right, right in my gut feeling. He had been speaking to her - again, another injustice I could rage about.

"You're on a downward spiral", Dad said to me. DENIAL hit me like a ton weight. I was in sheer disgust that Dad, my number one champion and supporter, would ever speak to me in such a way. I was becoming a ghost in front him; I was existing with constant chaos and drama in my shadow.

My drinking habits were cemented at my friend's hen-do which went down the drain, and all because of me. I drank before the early train, and then proceeded to drink the spa out of Prosecco. I honestly, hand on heart, didn't care for anyone else but my drink that day, it was all about me and not about my dear friend, who continues to deserve the earth and more.

The Botanist was our next stop of the day, and my final one. I was refused the right to drink on the premise, I was escorted out after calling the barman a CUNT and trying to pay only £0.87 for the meal... but I wasn't in the wrong, everyone else was. Just like my disease the situation was cunning, powerful and baffling. My friend ushered me into a cab and before I knew it Belle was calling; my dad had been informed.

I ruined my best friend's hen-do yet I was enraged with anger at how I was mistreated. Work that one out. Yep, you'd think I'd have my tail in between legs with the shame and guilt, but no I felt like I was owed an apology.

It only expedited my drinking, fuelling my physical need to continue sipping on the devil's poison. My 26th birthday went out with a traditional bang, it started with me receiving a letter from my brother expressing his need to cut communication with me due to my drinking, again I reacted with anger, how dare he?! I blamed him for how that evening unfolded...

My eating disorder was out to play again, I felt huge, like a blown-up version of myself, so that just intensified matters. I drank, no cocaine, just liquid gold for me. I thought it would be a great idea to hit the town with the girls. Like lady muck, I thought I could walk straight into the club because my ex used to work there. I was sent back out, and again the injustice sent me north west, I lost it.

I saw red, things escalated and before I knew it 5 coppers were restraining me on the ground, I was chucked into a riot van (yes, The Artic Monkey's come to mind), and carted off to the cop shop. There I continued to ring the buzzer, demanding nicotine etc. They asked if I was alcohol dependent, I laughed of course I wasn't, yet a unfathomable feeling in my gut confirmed I was. Upon being discharged with a drunk & disorderly, I went straight to the Co-op to get some wine before grabbing a cab back to Belle's.

She told me she loved me, but said it was time for me to head back to Dad's, he had demanded I go home. How was I going to worm myself out of this one? It was then mutually agreed that I would go back to Ireland for a period of time to get back on track.

The Emerald Isle brought countless amounts of wine-walks; I would buy bottles of rosé to convince myself I wasn't an alcoholic because they only drank the hard stuff. I physically couldn't eat, listening to Adele's "Easy on Me" on repeat as I walked miles around the country lanes.

My grandparents were diamonds as always, trying to be there for me, I tried to convince my granny I wasn't an alcoholic - who does that if they're not in denial? My time in Ireland consisted of drinking, walking and sleeping. I stole countless bottles of spirits from their drink's trolley, distilling the vodka ones with water.

There's often a joke about the 'ghost' at my granny and granda's - that ghost is me. The Lent after I stayed there Granda asked for a drink, Granny made him a vodka soda but as he took one sip, he urged my tee-total Granny to try it. It was H_2O, she'd only chosen one of my secretive bottles. My thinking was anyone who uses it would probably be pissed and none the wiser!

During this stint in Ireland, I soon made the informed decision to stay at my aunt's in Dublin so I'd be closer to the shop and less likely to be monitored. I started to hit up Tinder whilst away, I got ghosted on a date, so I proceeded to drink two bottles of wine at a restaurant on my own. I was pissed as a fart by the time my auntie collected me, I'd already consumed God knows how many beers before leaving for this supposed date.

I have to say I missed living with Belle, two gingers, one sausage dog and a bed. It was bliss, I managed to hide the extent of my drinking from her, I sadly manipulated her to my hymn tune, she was oblivious to just how much I was drinking. It was hidden in plain sight. Yet she has stuck by me through thick and thin.

A funny moment which gave me a rare belly laugh was one occasion when we ordered Domino's. The delivery driver arrived but had dropped our big dip. Before we knew it he was back with a free pizza and extra big dip, he then proceeded to chat Belle up. I was in hysterics. She's since moved, and he's delivered to her new address. It's the little things, isn't it?

CHAPTER 8

BALLS AND A DETOX

"Sometimes it takes an overwhelming breakdown to have an undeniable breakthrough"

UNKNOWN

Balls and a detox, that's how I'm going to introduce this next chapter... I'll set the scene of that fatal night, the one that finally sent me hurtling towards rock bottom. Belle and I had gone for drinks in Warwick, of course I had no reservations, that on this occasion, I'd only be having a 'couple' of drinks. Sadly, that imaginary sense of hope diminished, I was at the local off license buying extra drinks just for the hell of it all.

We soon headed back to hers, I wanted the party to continue, I physically hadn't had enough to drink, I needed more. With the decadent taste of each sip came the obsession of my next drink. I was always ahead of time, planning on what, when and how I'd successfully obtain my next liquid gold.

Whilst at Belle's I felt this sense of injustice, that she was cock blocking me from a drink, and that wouldn't do. I was adamant that I was going home and, bless her, she was losing an uphill battle. That's the thing with me, when it came to booze, nothing would stop me in my tracks, I was a woman on a mission.

Belle, with all the best intentions in the world, tried to stop me from leaving, from driving drunk, but I managed to overpower her. I got in the car with the dog, unrelenting I reversed straight into a wooden fence, praying I would get home albeit I was intoxicated.

A Nina Nesbitt track came on in my car, one I greatly related to my ex, and then it hit me... I had lost him, there was no more me and him, and a familiar dark cloud circled over me. As I neared toward my home, somehow successfully manoeuvring my car through the dark streets, I became overwhelmed with a dreaded suicidal urge.

A combination of self-hatred and despair inflicted all of my being. This was it; time to successfully finish the job. I was ready to eradicate all the pain, all the fog and distress I had caused those I loved.

In my self-centred pursuit, I gave zero shits about the dog, she was just an innocent bystander in it all. I unclipped my seatbelt before aiming directly for a tree.

BOOM, before I knew it the car had flipped, I remember hearing my Bluetooth ringing, it was Belle, I was unable to answer it. I was perplexed, completely unaware of how and what my actions had resulted in.

All of a sudden, I could hear a man's voice, he was trying to keep me conscious by talking to me. He happened to be a neighbour who was coincidently walking his dog. As a retired fireman he was well aware of how to approach and handle the situation. But in that moment, all I cared about was the dog, my beloved Lottie, what had I done to her?

After I was cut out of the car, my roadside breath test was taken, my reading was 4.5 times over the limit. I don't remember this happening. I have a vague memory of being in the ambulance, seeing my sister and screaming at her to look after the dog.

She happened to be walking home when she noticed the road was closed with my distinctive car upside down in the middle of it. I don't know if I'll ever forgive myself for putting her through such a trauma, after losing Tiarnan the way we did.

You see the car landed pretty much by the top of our family road, it must have been an ordeal for her, but she kindly took the dog to the emergency vet and made sure she was ok.

I was ushered off in the ambulance, convoy intact with the police following behind. In a matter of moments, I'd arrived at the all too familiar A&E of my local hospital. Two policemen accompanied me as I was brought to a separate cubicle, and boy did they get some shit from me.

After various scans and tests, the overseeing doctor deemed me medically fit enough to provide a second sample for them. I refused to give them the requested blood sample, my ego inflated, I wasn't going to reap the repercussions of my actions, what had I done so wrong?

Much to my surprise, and God sent luck, the nurse who had overseen my brother's fatality was on shift. A kind, humble lady who refers to that day as one she'll never forget. Upon recognising me, she ensured I calmed down, keeping me in line especially when interacting with the police. She witnessed them 'de-arresting' me, and who could blame them for doing so? I'd thrown enough verbal shit their way.

All of a sudden both my dad and sister appeared. They had come to collect me following my pending discharge, I was counting the moments until I'd have some form of liquor creeping down my throat. I only sustained a broken nose, ribs and a head injury along with the usual whiplash, a fragment of the injuries I should have endured. Nothing a bit of booze would anaesthetise.

As soon as I got home, it was 'Wine O'clock', sure it was 5pm somewhere. My sister exploded using some choice words to describe my actions and my drinking tendencies.

I dismissed her completely. I needed oblivion more than I needed her lecture. I was faced with limbo, battered and bruised I was a broken woman. I found myself curled in bed next to the dog, painfully sinking as much wine as I physically could.

As I slipped into reality the following morning, I found myself at my GP Surgery with Dad. It was agreed that I was immediately referred to the local CGL group, a recovery partnership.

There was no running from things, it was literally located opposite the doctors. After providing an overview of my drinking career, it was recommended that I began reducing my alcohol units by 10% every 3 days. The amount I was consuming meant it wasn't safe for me to physically just stop, I was a 24/7 drinker.

Dad, God bless him, monitored and managed my alcohol consumption, but little did he know that I had booze hidden around the house! I wasn't going to go quietly into an alcohol reduced situation. Pops went to Majestic to get cheap bottles of wine, he didn't want to use his 'expensive' stuff, what was the point? I was going to stop, wasn't I?

In the wreckage of the accident, my phone was catapulted into a hidden area of the written off vehicle. Phoneless, I contacted my nearest and dearest from my iPad, but some of them were already aware.

Unbeknown to me, the police had released a Facebook post which outlined the details of the event with a photo of my uniquely coloured car and a distinctive road in the background. It wasn't hard for those who knew me to put 2+2 together. I was the last one to the coming out party of my alcoholism - everyone knew before me.

Sadly, the 'Boys in Blue Part Two' was about to unfold. The Monday after the accident, I lost it at my dad, he refused to give me anymore alcohol, I had consumed my daily limit. My sisters got involved and sadly got the brunt of my acid tongue, but I levelled up to the next stage, I began to become physical. As a last resort, my dad urged my sisters to ring the police.

They promptly arrived, they were two young good-looking lads, and for some reason I sobered up. I engaged with them, normally I'd be spewing that they're cunts, offloading my harboured anger toward them. Their sargeant said, given I was calm and cooperative, that they could leave, but any other calls to the house would lead to me being arrested.

Why couldn't they understand I was in desperate need of alcohol, with that in hand all would be grand. That's all my insular world required, that and a snuggle from the dog. Then Wednesday came, I woke up with a different mindset. I had tried, whilst pissed, a few Zoom AA Meetings, but don't ask me how they went, I can't remember them in the slightest.

That morning, I hit my rock bottom, I was done, I was throwing the towel in. I was finally sick and tired of being sick and tired.

I wasn't sure how to stop, and with drinking over 40 units a day, I was in dangerous territory. I called an ambulance, to this day I still don't know if they came or if Pops brought me to A&E.

It now feels like a mirage, 2.5 years later it pains me to write about this, my emotional rock bottom was by far the most pain I have endured. It was as if I was walking from Hell to Heaven, along hot stones, or saying goodbye to my dearest of best friends. It was time, time to get better, and this was the only way I knew how. It was my last resort.

In my obliterated haze, I recall seeing a friend's mum working on reception at A&E. In sheer kindness she ushered on the process of me being seen and receiving treatment. I vaguely recollect meeting the Alcohol Liaison Officer before being moved to a further two wards. Eventually I was transferred to Castle Ward, where the remainder of my detox continued.

Before my admission, Hayley and Belle had come to Dad's with a McDonalds for me. Inside my Happy Meal came a 'Mr Bumpy' toy, he was my cheerleader all throughout my hospital admission, I still have him to this day. He gave me something I had lacked for an eternity, 'hope'. I had to hope now, I had to persevere and trust in the process, I was finally done.

Aside from Dad none of my siblings visited me in hospital, and I don't blame them. At the time, I was full of resentment, I was bemused as to why they wouldn't come and see their sister, but I was in victim mode. This was something I had to do for myself, and in time those around me would learn to trust and love me again.

During my time on the ward, I stopped eating meat, I lost my appetite apart from butter mint sweets and fizzy drinks. Over those painful 9 days, I took up smoking again, chasing the feeling of what was now a distant drink. I was sneaking a vape in my cubicle at night as well, all to distract from my overpowering desires to drink.

I don't miss the horrendous shaking; the sweats; the dry retching; being sick and the flu like symptoms. It was part of the process though, it was imperative that I went through these stages, it's sad that it had gotten so far.

At times, I was so tempted to go to the local shop to buy a bottle of vodka. All my debit cards had been taken off me, but I still had the luxury of Apple Pay. I recall calling Dad, shouting how desperate I was for a drink, you see the obsession was still on me, it hadn't lifted at this point.

Molly, Laura, Belle and Hayley each visited me, and that was worth its weight in gold, I can never thank them enough for their love and support. The girls came armed with things like fresh pjs and sweet treats, but ultimately their presence was all I needed. I am so fortunate to have women like these in my life, still present after all they'd experienced and endured from my bullshit ways.

Time went painfully slow, I was crippled physically and emotionally with anxiety, what was the next stage to welcome? Before I knew it, I was being discharged, I was prescribed Acamprosate to manage my cravings of the booze. As mentioned before, my first stint in rehab introduced me to AA, and I knew it was the only and last place for me to turn to.

The only way to maintain going forward was to engage with the 12-step fellowship. I knew in my heart it was the right thing to do. I honestly, hand on heart, didn't want to drink again, I was scared, bemused if you will. I was a deer in headlights, how was I to navigate my recovery when all I could think about was booze...

I attended my first meeting on a Saturday night, black and blue, nose and ribs broken I entered the room. There was a sea of smiles, I was confused, these people didn't look like drunks and they were happy? How the fuck did that work out? They were sober.

I didn't appreciate the joy sobriety would give me at that point. I listened, I listened for the similarities not the differences. I shared, I shared about what had happened to me, it was a relief, these people understood me. I wasn't an outcast.

I quickly learnt the importance of Sponsorship; I remember hearing my sponsor for the first time on a Tuesday. Christ, she spoke of an eating disorder (tick), she was young (tick) and she was a daily drinker (I've hit the jackpot here)! Her story had some differences, but what mainly transpired was she had what I wanted, she was exactly where I wanted to be; sober.

So, I asked her out, yep, asking a Sponsor is almost like asking someone out on a date. It was a Friday evening, I just word vomited it out, "will you be my Sponsor?", and the rest is history. Don't get me wrong, there have been times when I've wanted to throw the Big Book at her.

I never for a second imagined I would meet new found friends for life within the rooms. People welcomed me, they opened their arms and ears to listen to me, even when I was so manic in the early days. I would drink copious amounts of tea with sugar as I exchanged similar dialogues with likeminded people.

This would occur on a daily basis, I would attend a meeting nearly every day of the week, I wasn't jeopardising my abstinence from booze. You see, for me, the real work hadn't started as of yet, I hadn't commenced with the 12-steps straight away, the day I did was when my real sobriety began.

I did fall into a clique at the time, and this proved to be a lesson within itself. You see people in the rooms are unwell, and sometimes I would lose sight of this. We are each on our own journeys, and it's important for me to stick with the winners, those actively working a program. I now have a tribe of people I surround myself with, people with REAL recovery. It's easy to get lost amongst those who are unwell. That's not to say I'm well or have this stuff sussed.

My first stick in the old road, was flirting with the idea of my ex. Yep, he soon returned in my early recovery, I can see that God welcomed him back into my life for a number of reasons. One was to make my amends. I teased the future of my sobriety by seeing him intoxicated. He was almost always sideways when I saw him. We would cry, have sex and listen to our songs - yes Lucy Rose, I will give you a shoutout, your whole ‘Like I Used To’ album defined our relationship.

Our walk along Newbold Comyn was where I made my Step 9 amendments, I apologised for all my recounted wrongdoing. It was raw and emotional to say the least, I was finally owning my own shit, I was releasing all the pent-up resentment, fear and shame.

The bit that broke my heart the most was the painful pleasantries of selling our house. The process wasn’t easy nor was it cheap. I stood there for the last time, all by myself, amongst the bricks and mortar which I presumed would be the first of many homes for us. I earned some perspective that day, as I sobbed from the pit of my stomach. It wasn’t the end of an era, but the end of me and him, it was time to close the chapter. No more us, it was just me and the dog now.

In absolute despair, I spoke to my Sponsor; she encouraged me to go to a meeting. At that point I was willing to do anything, I was (and hopefully still remain) teachable. As I went, I shut the door and locked it. That was my final experience in that house, I was sober.

CHAPTER 9

SHAMEFUL SERENADES

"One Day at a Time"

AA

Hail Hayley', yes my darling crocodile to whom this book is dedicated. She is one of my soul sisters, and the very reason for me embarking on this writing journey. She kindly reminded me during the darkest of my sobriety difficulties, that I could cultivate how I felt through the power of writing.

I have always enjoyed writing, it is a form of expression, a way to offload the shit, and find common denominators with others. I began writing my blog back when I was 21 years old, it was during my active battle with anorexia (yes, stay tuned folks, there MAY be another book!).

To celebrate the milestone of being 1 year sober I headed to New York. I couldn't believe it, I was in one of my favourite places, attending an AA meeting on the other side of the globe. It just showed me how large the 12-step fellowship is. Receiving my one-year chip was surreal, I was surrounded by likeminded but total strangers, who couldn't have been happier for me.

In true celebratory fashion, one of my character defects came out, the old impulsive spending. I treated myself to a MacBook to congratulate myself, and with that I hit the keypad in little old Brooklyn reactivating my old blog. It was a relief, I was able to relay recent events all the while diluting my shame, guilt and ego.

I couldn't believe the reception, people were so supportive, others reached out seeking advice. It's important to note, everything in the rooms (the Program) is but a suggestion, no-one is an authority or God, it's about the magic of one alcoholic conversing with another.

Quickly, lovewhatmatters.com picked up my story, they published it and the snowball continued. A PR company sold it to the Mirror and Chat Magazine. Seen Stories published a video summarising my rock bottom and recovery journey.

I was overwhelmed, utterly gobsmacked that my story was getting some airtime, and for that I'm grateful. Particularly in hope it would help at least one person, but primarily those of the younger generation. For right or wrong, I'm a very open book, I'm transparent; after all the program for this fear-based condition is cemented on rigorous honesty.

In turn, this led to the rebranding of 'Searching for Sersh' - it would be rude to not play on an alliteration. I worked with my friend on the rebrand, praising the Lord for the use of Canva. It's bloody fantastic, and easy to navigate. It's a page dedicated to sobriety in both senses of my eating disorder and alcoholism. It's also important to note, it's a work in progress as I've had to focus on my Step Work.

The 1,2,3 waltz happened rather early in my recovery, I hit the ground running with the first 3 steps. I had a solid Step 1, boy am I powerless over alcohol. I knew in my heart I could never drink again, and that, for me, was the difference in admitting and accepting my malady. I can also admit that my life was utterly unmanageable and it still can be today.

Step 2 didn't cause me any difficulty, during my drinking I prayed, I prayed every night in hope that God would listen to my requests. Gosh, it brings me back to the darkness, the desire to drink tapered by a sense of minimal willingness to stop. I've always believed that there's something greater than me, a Higher Power (or God), after all how have I survived such a shit storm?

Step 3 was slightly conflicting for me, I was so ready for something else to deal with my shit, but equally I feared the loss of control. I had spent the majority of my life controlling the show; controlling how I felt with booze and food; manipulating people so they stuck to my script… how was I supposed to sacrifice control now?

Easy, through the guidance of my Sponsor and fellows' experiences. I remained teachable, I gave this a chance, after all the definition of insanity is to constantly repeat the same thing while expecting a different outcome.

Before I knew it, Step 4 was on the cards and boy did it open my eyes and ears. I was to be fearless, and thorough; I chose an alternative approach - a life story of those I held the greatest resentments for. It was liberating, freeing and God damn informative.

I held the mirror directly opposite me, I dissected situations, measuring my part played in scenarios I had originally felt innocent in. I unearthed my character defects for what they were, deflating my ego bit by bit.

I must say, I shared my Step 5 with both my Sponsor and another fellow. This occurred simply by fate, my Higher Power invited the opportunity for me to share with two trusted parties. It's commonly said that 'you're only as sick as your darkest secret' and once I shared this, I unearthed more than words can describe, I instantly felt lighter.

A breath of fresh air, I could function at optimum, I had a taste of freedom so where Step 6 is concerned, I was ready to have my defects removed. I learnt my biggest downfall was self-seeking behaviour, and upon reflection I can see how my self-seeking behaviour landed me in dangerous situations. Sure, you've joined me on this journey so far, wouldn't you agree?

Asking God to remove my shortcomings was rather exciting for me, now I could see the wood for the trees and I was ready. I was ready to exorcise my demons, to eradicate my downfalls.

It is difficult parting with defects, they're old habits, default behaviours which I have found hard to disengage with. One that I've worked incredibly hard on is my swearing, and from fellows' feedback I have succeeded in minimising it, people would even comment that I'm well spoken.

Appropriate apologies (Step 8 & 9) were next on my list, I named all those I owed amends to, the list included people I had lost contact with. To my nearest and dearest I continue to make my daily amends by remaining sober, and over time I trust they'll become less sceptical of my recovery.

By this I mean that after 10+ years of the drinking chaos I cultivated, it's understandably hard to forgive and forget. Time is the greatest healer, and I intend, one day a time, to choose recovery each and every day.

A few letters were sent to those I owed amends to, on the basis that it wouldn't cause harm to them or I. I sent these under no pretence or hope of receiving a response. I honestly was more reluctant about having difficult conversations with my friends, but nevertheless I invited the opportunity to do so.

It was key for me to sit back and listen, to digest my wrongdoings and the way I had hurt each individual one. This wasn't about me; it was about them and how my drinking had detrimentally affected them.

Daily abstinence alongside my 12-step program is how I continue to repair my relationships. I am slowly regaining the trust of my nearest and dearest, but Rome wasn't built in a day so practising patience and persevering with the process is part of my daily ritual. I no longer need to hide bottles, there are no bottles, I no longer have to isolate nor do I have to lie.

I still get myself involved in bizarre situations at the best of times, such as getting cash from a drug dealer. It was my first sober Christmas; I was with the girls on the hunt for a Christmas tree for Belle. Of course, the farm only accepted cash, so in a desperate need of some we went to the nearest corner shop. They didn't do cashback; however, the shop attendant was a local drug dealer with copious amounts of cash on him.

In true Sersh fashion I flirted with the idea of doing a bank transfer which he accepted. For once I wasn't picking up a 20 bag from a dealer, just 20 quid for a festive essential for my best friend. Off we went on our jollies, yes, we got the tree and it looked delightful.

CHAPTER 10

THE ART OF NOT RUINING EVERYONE'S LIVES

"People often say that motivation doesn't last. Neither does bathing. That's why we recommend it daily"

Zig Ziglar

My life has changed all for the better; it has transcended into a 4th-dimension I never knew possible. I have grown up, and I have had to change my priorities, first and foremost, my recovery is number one. My week consists of 2-3 meetings and visits with my Sponsor and Sponsee (Step 12). I like to spice things up by going to a mixture of 'Step' and 'Experience, Strength and Hope' ones; the variety adds to my wealth of endless learning.

I've learnt that 'service' is so important; it is a fundamental part of recovery. I've acquired several different service positions, such as treasurer and making the teas and coffees. On days when I don't feel like attending a meeting, it gets me there. It encourages me to actively participate in the fellowship; it opens a door of conversation with newcomers - the most important people in the rooms.

Step 10 is a daily practice for me; I ensure I do my personal inventory each and every day. It's a reminder to check in with myself, to look at my part in situations, thus making amends with anyone I may have harmed. Importantly, it also shines a light on the good deeds I've done within that particular day.

I'm slowly becoming better at calling myself out on my bullshit, which has been a blessing to do so in real-time. The power of the 'pause' - how do I respond to a situation as opposed to react? Does my ego need to be inflated by casting references to sexual innuendos during a perfectly normal conversation?

'Life on life's terms' is one of the common slogans used in the rooms. Life has well and truly been happening for me in sobriety; I suffered my first loss, my great aunt Meg, she was a doll and a true lady. It was so sad, she suffered a stroke, which was cruel in itself, as she'd previously lost her husband to one. She kindly left us some inheritance, which assisted with making my financial amends.

Much more recently, I had to grieve my uncle Killian; we tragically lost him in a workplace accident. It broke my heart, especially when my second cousin relayed just how proud of me he was, that he had shared my podcast with her, in his words, I was 'deadly'.

Interestingly, this unimaginable event welcomed my mother back into my life for all of 5 minutes. It was her brother who had passed. Between the therapy and 12-step work I've committed to, I was able to treat her as an unwell woman who needed serious help. To the best of my ability, I didn't allow her to phase me, after all, why allow someone to live in your head rent-free? So, I prayed, I prayed for her that she finds peace. After all, resentments are the biggest killer for us alcoholic folk, so I did what many before me have done and still continue to do so.

Aside from the dog being diagnosed with terminal cancer, my beautiful, constant companion, I believe this was my biggest trigger in recovery. Temporarily having to invite her back into my space (my safe space in Ireland) wasn't easy, but I had to continue having acceptance around the situation. After all, I know the pain the loss of a brother brings, regardless of how long they hadn't spoken.

Grief is a funny thing; the stages you go through are like a whirlwind, and they hit you unexpectedly, almost in a haunting sense. For me, it's about accepting my new reality, that sadly, the person is but a memory and that's why I prioritise making memories with those I love, after all, that's all we have.

Temporary triggers, such as eating disorder habits, have reappeared with new introductions, such as binging without the purging. I've been in this push-and-pull situation whereby I find myself binging on shit but not compensating for it. Again, it's me trying to fill the hole in the soul, to change the way I feel.

Ultimately, between this newfound behaviour and medication, I have increased in size, which makes my skin crawl. It's been a battle for me, especially now I have my license back.

Whilst I was carless, I was walking an excess of 13+ miles a day, with no real weight loss effect, and this is most certainly down to my medication, after all, I'm retaining 77% water at present.

Triggering or what for someone whose head is continually filled with darling Anorexia's words. To top it off, I've also been diagnosed with chronic fatigue syndrome (ME), so those extra steps really fuelled my exhaustion.

Just shy of a year since my near-fatal car crash, I found myself in court for 'failure to supply a second specimen'. It was time to face the music, to own up to my actions and to deal with the consequences.

My Higher Power was watching over me; I was given a 12-month suspension and a fine, I know people who'd done less and received a higher sentence than me. My solicitor quickly ushered me out of the court before they could change their minds.

I was entitled to get my license back from June 2023 as I'd completed a Drink Driving Course, which allowed me a 3-month sentence reduction. It did take an absolute age to get my license back, but between various tests and meetings, Friday 13th October 2023 came and I was granted it back. Again, I was blessed with another lesson in patience from my Higher Power.

I originally planned this chapter over a year ago, and I can tell you, that things have changed dramatically since then. I failed to mention how my self-seeking behaviour excelled. I was getting my ego stroked by multiple Tinder flings; I was sleeping with 3-4 guys a week, thinking I was lady muck. I was searching for something in sex; it was about exerting my power and control, my desire to be wanted and needed.

Then I stumbled upon this Irish guy, who I frankly asked on the first date if we'd be having sex, ultimately we did. In my head, I needed to outline what it was, if it was going to be casual or not. It wasn't until Laur asked me to give it a go with one of my flings that I asked him out on a date-date, and well, the rest is history!

There was something about him; he was level-headed, hard-working, handsome and pretty much tee-total. He only had one pint on our first date, which amazed me, I still get baffled by how people drink 'normally', that they can have one and call it a day.

It's safe to say my boyfriend is a mysterious fella, he can be hard to read at the best of times, but over time both of us have allowed our guards to come down. Being in a new relationship, a far healthier one than my previous, has been an eye-opener but an equal trigger as well. My Borderline Personality Disorder has flared up at times due to fears that I have allowed to fester. These moments have been easily rectified through communication, something I never used to do.

At times, I find myself comparing the relationship to my old one, the difference is I was in active addiction back then. Today, it is different, and experiencing a sober relationship is eye-opening. From feelings to intimate moments, it's like an epiphany, something you navigate through without the drama and chaos.

I have to remind myself that I am loveable, I am worthy of respect, love and intimacy. I continue to work closely with my inner child to gently engulf her with all the ingredients of the healthy relationships she lacked.

I and my love now live together, another blessing I have received in my recovery, it's been a dream so far, I actually feel at home, which is a far cry from my previous house.

I've also found myself navigating my way around the world slowly but surely, I have travelled to places such as Milan and Geneva, did I mention I've done some solo trips. After all, this wouldn't be possible without working on my program, and it meant I could finally do something for myself.

For years, I dulled my mind with intoxicating liquor; I became disinterested in life, cultures, places and people. Travelling has opened me up to new experiences, giving me food for thought, a conversation opener and insight.

I've also travelled around the country, seeing friends, creating memories and attending meetings. It's a wealth of experience I have accumulated so far in such a short space of time. Little did I intend to cross paths with the Soroptimists - a volunteer movement empowering and supporting girls and women on a global scale.

Without the Soroptimists, I wouldn't have been granted the Diamond Education Grant, which financially supported my writer's coach, Ali - without her, this wouldn't have been possible. I would be clueless, and this book may never have been written. I'm indebted to this group of ladies who support local initiatives and charities.

Thank you to Dishi for all her continued support; she has been a cheerleader of mine, and for that, I'm grateful. The link deepens, I wouldn't have been introduced to her without the support of Catherine Williamson.

Catherine's Daughter was best friends with my brother at school; her son was also in my sister's year. She had stumbled upon some of my writing on Facebook and reconnected with me. She is an inspiring lady, one who echoes knowledge and wisdom through her successful podcast "Gobsmacked!".

Kindly, she invited me to record an episode with her - 'Sober'. It touched on some of the difficulties I endeavoured, which led me to drink and, of course, the crash. It was a new platform for me to communicate my journey with listeners, gaining first listens in Cambodia, Saint-Martin, Loas and Hungary. What an experience! I recall being nervous but equally excited to spread the message. After all, AA is about attraction, not promotion.

I've been blessed and afforded with so many opportunities since I surrendered. It's been cathartic writing this memoir sharing with you some of my darkest, rawest moments. I continue to practice my daily prayers and meditation (Step 11), without them, I'd lack direction and guidance, after all, I have to hand over my will to my Higher Power.

For anyone struggling, it's never too early to commence on a journey in sobriety; you aren't too young or old. Nothing in this life is linear, when shit hits the fan, check in with yourself - are you hungry, angry, lonely or tired? I also apply D.I.Y to most things - 'don't involve yourself' - the art of not giving a fuck is a beautiful one, who knows, maybe one day I'll master it.

For today, one day at a time, I will not drink; I will be of service, and I will live. I choose life. Peace & Love xx

ACKNOWLEDGEMENTS

Catherine, without writing that initial Facebook post, the Gobsmacked! Podcast episode wouldn't have birthed and the multitude of opportunities and contacts I have endeavoured since wouldn't be a thing.

Dishi, your zest for life and connecting people was anything but detrimental to me. I would never have been introduced to the Soroptimists and Ali without these connections.

Ali, you've been my ride or die throughout this process, far more than a Writer's Coach, a guiding influence and supporter even when I doubted myself the most.

Lastly, my nearest and dearest and of course my Honey - you know who you are 'xo

SPONSORS & SUPPORTERS

This book has been written thanks to the support of Soroptimists International.

A charitable organisation, Soroptimist International Great Britain and Ireland (SIGBI) has 6000 Members in 270 Clubs in 18 countries including Great Britain, Ireland and countries in Asia, the Caribbean and Malta, who work at a local, national and international level to educate, empower and enable women and girls.

Soroptimists work to help improve the lives of women and girls worldwide, using their networks to deliver projects relevant in their own localities and universally. Many of the problems facing women and girls are the same everywhere, for example gender inequality, but there are particular problems in each continent, country, region and locality.

Saoirse's book was part funded by SIGBI as a project to help inform young people about the dangers of alcoholism and untreated trauma and ultimately resilience in the face of these obstacles.

RESOURCES

Soroptimists International Great Britain and Ireland - For membership or support enquiries https://sigbi.org/

NHS - The NHS in the UK offers various services for drug and alcohol abuse. You can contact your local NHS trust or visit the NHS website for information on addiction services. https://www.nhs.uk/live-well/addiction-support/

Alcoholics Anonymous (AA) UK - women who share their experience, strength, and hope with each other to help solve their common problem and help others to recover from alcoholism. For local meetings and contact information:
https://www.alcoholics-anonymous.org.uk/

Narcotics Anonymous (NA) UK - NA is a non-profit fellowship of men and women for whom drugs have become a major problem. https://ukna.org

Talk to Frank - Frank is a UK-based service providing confidential advice and information about drugs.
https://www.talktofrank.com

Mind - Mind is a mental health charity in the UK. While not specific to substance abuse, they can provide information and support for mental health issues, which may include trauma.
https://www.mind.org.uk

Release - Release is a national centre of expertise on drugs and drug laws. They

provide free and confidential advice on drugs and the law.
https://www.release.org.uk

Adfam - Adfam is a national charity working with families affected by drugs and alcohol.
https://adfam.org.uk

When seeking support, it's also advisable to contact your local GP (General Practitioner) or healthcare provider, as they can provide guidance and refer you to appropriate services in your area.

Contact me!

Instagram:

SAOIRSENIAMH95

[illegible]RSERSHSERENADE

Email: lottiepublishingco@gmail.com

Website: www.searchingforsersh.wordpress.com

Printed in Great Britain
by Amazon

50040988R00109